THE
2nd
WIND

COMPILED BY BEST-SELLING AUTHORS
DR. JOAN T RANDALL & LESLIE J COTTRELL

THE
2nd
WIND

INSPIRING STORIES OF RESILIENCE, RENEWAL AND REINVENTION IN LIFE'S LATER YEARS!

VICTORIOUS YOU PRESS

Published by Victorious You Press™

Charlotte NC, USA

TITLE: THE 2ND WIND

First Printed: 2025

Editor: Charmaine Castillo

Cover Designer: Jadia Bellamy

ISBN: 978-1-959719-51-9

ISBN: (eBook) 978-1-959719-52-6

Library of Congress Control Number: 2025902845

Printed in the United States of America

For details email joan@victoriousyoupress.com
or visit us at www.victoriousyoupress.com

DEDICATION

To the resilient souls who have faced life's storms yet found the strength to rise again—this book is for you.

To those who have endured setbacks, heartbreaks, and unexpected detours but refused to be defined by them—may *THE 2ND WIND* remind you that your story isn't over; it's just entering a new chapter.

To the dreamers, the believers, and the overcomers—may this anthology serve as a beacon of hope, igniting the courage within you to embrace your *2ND WIND* with boldness, faith, and unwavering determination.

And to the One who gives us the breath of life and the strength to press forward—thank You for being our ever-present source of renewal and grace.

ACKNOWLEDGEMENTS

Bringing *THE 2ND WIND* to life has been a journey of faith, resilience, and unwavering collaboration.

To our phenomenal contributing authors—thank you for your courage in sharing your stories of perseverance and triumph. Your words will serve as a guiding light for those searching for strength in their own seasons of transition.

To Rachel Reed, Charmaine LaFondé, Jadia Bellamy, and Nadia Monsano–our publishing partners and creative team—your dedication and expertise have shaped this project into a masterpiece. Your belief in the power of storytelling has made this anthology a reality.

To our family, friends, and supporters—your encouragement, prayers, and belief in this vision have carried us through every step of this process. Your love has been our anchor.

To every reader who turns these pages—may you find the inspiration, wisdom, and faith to embrace your own *2ND WIND*. You are stronger than you know, and the best is yet to come.

With Love and Gratitude

TABLE OF CONTENTS

INTRODUCTION   1

SECTION I: FINDING THE MISSING PUZZLE PIECE   3

THE POWER OF HIS DEATH   5

THE JOURNEY BACK TO HER   13

IT'S HELL IN THE HALLWAY   23

PURPOSE DEFIES AGE   33

DROWNING IN MY PLACE OF COMFORT   43

FINALLY FREE TO FIND ME   53

SECTION II: FROM SHADOWS TO LOVE'S LIGHT   63

STRIPPED TO THE SOUL   65

REBIRTH OF THE QUEEN   75

RELEASED FROM THE SHACKLES OF A BROKEN COVENANT   85

BETRAYED BY LOVE   95

DELIVERED FROM THE VALLEY OF THE UNKNOWN   105

THE BOW AND ARROW COVENANT   115

ABOUT THE AUTHORS   127

NIKEMA BRYANT   129

ANGELA M MITCHELL   130

KRISTY BUSIJA   131

CHARMAINE LAFONDÉ   132

CHRISTAL SPENCE NEWKIRK   133

SHARON R THOMPSON   134

LESLIE J COTTRELL   135

REGINA NICHELLE   136

ROBIN A. HILL   138

SARA OMAYA AGAK   140

LISA RICHMOND   141

Dr. JOAN T RANDALL   143

INTRODUCTION

There are moments in life when it feels as if the rug has been pulled right out from under you—when everything you've built, everything you've known, comes crashing down in an instant. I know this feeling intimately. I lost everything and had to start over, facing a reality that seemed both cruel and unavoidable. The weight of uncertainty sat heavy on my chest, and for a moment, I wondered if I would ever regain my footing.

Then, I had a conversation with my dear friend Leslie, only to find out she had experienced the very same thing. Different circumstances, but the same gut-wrenching reality—life as she knew it had changed, and she, too, had to rebuild. As we talked, we realized we weren't alone. This wasn't just our story; this was *a story*—a universal experience shared by so many. Life has a way of forcing us into transitions we never expected, of stripping away comfort so we can uncover a deeper strength within.

But one thing became clear: life was not over. We were not finished. In fact, we had been given something invaluable—a second wind. This time, we weren't just surviving; we were choosing to *thrive*. Armed with the lessons from our past, we made a conscious decision to chart a new course, not as the people we once were, but as wiser, stronger versions of ourselves. We realized that starting over wasn't a punishment; it was an opportunity.

This time, we vowed to love ourselves first, to fill our tanks until they overflowed, so that when we gave to others, it was from abundance and not depletion. No longer would we pour from a near-empty cup, running on fumes and neglecting our own needs. Instead, we embraced a new way of living—one rooted in self-care, intentionality, and the belief that our next chapter would be the best yet.

That is the heart of *THE 2ND WIND*.

This anthology is a collection of stories from individuals who, like us, faced the unimaginable and came out on the other side— not just standing, but soaring. Each story is a testament to resilience, to reinvention, and to the undeniable power of a fresh start. These pages hold the wisdom of those who refused to be defined by their losses and instead used them as fuel for a greater comeback.

So, if you find yourself in a season where everything seems uncertain, where life has shifted in ways you never anticipated, know this: you are not alone. Your story isn't over. In fact, this just might be the moment you step into your own second wind—the moment where you reclaim your power, rewrite the narrative, and embrace the future that's waiting for you.

Welcome to *THE 2ND WIND*. May these stories inspire you, uplift you, and remind you that sometimes, losing everything is the first step to gaining so much more.

FINDING THE MISSING PUZZLE PIECE

"God, pick up the pieces. Put me back together again. You are my praise!" Jeremiah 17:14 MSG

THE POWER OF HIS DEATH

NIKEMA BRYANT

Dwon Lamont Fields, Jr. ("DJ") was my only child, born on September 15, 2002. He was definitely not your average kid. When he was a little boy, I always heard people say, "He has an old soul," or "He has been here before," and that is how he carried himself. In his early years, DJ possessed the remarkable skill of participating in adult-level conversations, especially when those conversations centered around football. He was a huge Philadelphia Eagles and UGA Bulldog fan!

DJ always thought about others, and when you hear me say he would give the shoes off his feet, he literally did. When we were on vacation in Atlanta, DJ gave his shoes to a homeless man. He never liked seeing anyone sad or unhappy and always did his best to be that listening ear, shoulder to cry on, or be that person to make someone else smile. He was the kind of kid that any parent would have loved to have, but he was mine! We received compliments all the time from parents who expressed a desire to have the kind of relationship with their kid that I had with DJ, and a lot of his friends expressed the same sentiment concerning their desire to have a similar relationship with their mom.

We went on vacations together, went out to eat, watched movies, went shopping—the whole nine; we were like best friends. But although we had a unique dynamic in our mother/son relationship, I never let him forget who the mother was. DJ may have been an only child, but he was the big brother figure to all his friends. Many people have heard me say, "To be an only child, he sure has a lot of brothers and sisters!" Whenever he went out, I would ask him who he was going with, and he would always say, "My brother." Then I would ask, "Which one?" He was the mind of reasoning that his friends needed, even when he was the one telling them they were doing something wrong.

March 5, 2021, started out just like any other day. I went to DJ's room that morning to let him know I was headed to work. He was still in bed. He did not have a first period class that day, so he would be leaving the house later for school. We said our goodbyes and I was out the door.

Fishing was one of DJ's favorite hobbies, so later that afternoon when I got off from work, I called him to let him know I had found a new fishing spot for him.

"Cool, I'm going to have to check it out," he told me.

Then he let me know that he was going to Hilton Head with a couple of his friends for a while.

"Alright," I said. "See you when you get home."

DJ, his younger cousin, and a good friend of his, were out and about that afternoon riding around Hilton Head before stopping at a popular hangout spot for the local high-schoolers. They met up with some other friends to hang out in the parking lot (as they typically did). While hanging out, DJ was unaware that one of his friends was involved in an ongoing disagreement, and that those kids were on the prowl searching for his friend.

After leaving the hangout spot, DJ and his friends decided to cruise through town. While they were cruising around, DJ's car caught the attention of someone who mistakenly believed one of DJ's passengers was the person they were searching for. When they spotted his car, they informed their friends and gave the car's location. They began to follow DJ's car, but DJ had no idea he was being followed.

That night, at about 11:30 I received a phone call from DJ's dad calling to let me know that DJ had been involved in a car accident. My mind and my heart began to race. I thought about the deer that tend to run out in the road. I thought about whether or not DJ had been speeding. My mind was all over the place, and when I was finally able to speak, I asked, "Is he okay?"

His dad, who was out of town, did not know, so after ending the call, I jumped up, threw on some clothes, and drove to the accident scene. As I arrived at the scene, two fire trucks blocked the area. I quickly parked my car, ran to the other side of the street where DJ's car was, and began running toward it. A friend and her husband (who was a firefighter) stopped me. They had heard about the accident, which is why they were there. I saw DJ's car overturned on its side in a ditch, and I felt my stomach drop when I saw a white sheet covering a body lying in front of the car. By the shape of the sheet, I knew.

My baby, my son, my world, my reason for being, was gone. My heart literally broke into a million pieces. It was not supposed to be that way. The wannabe thugs that followed DJ's car for five minutes, thinking the person they were looking for was in there, pulled up alongside DJ's car and opened fire. DJ lost control of his vehicle, which ran off the road, hitting a cement housing development sign and ending up on its side in the ditch. DJ was in the driver's seat, his younger cousin was in the rear passenger seat, and his other friend was in the front passenger seat. The friend who was in the front passenger seat was able to get out of the car and call for help. Completely unaware of the casualty at that time, he thought DJ had just lost control of the vehicle.

Two days later, we still did not know why the shooting happened, especially why it happened to DJ. The authorities had no leads since DJ's passengers did not see the car that was involved in the shooting. The police asked me and DJ's father if we would be willing to do a TV interview to make an appeal to the public for answers or the whereabouts of the people who destroyed our lives, and, without hesitation, we agreed! Several news stations in our area broadcasted our story across the low county of South Carolina and Georgia as we pleaded for information that would lead to an arrest in our son's case. We urged anyone with information to come forward or contact the anonymous tip hotline to provide any details that could help us understand why this happened to our son.

DJ's dad was determined to get justice for DJ. He was at the police station every single day, waiting for any bit of information to come in. He followed up on leads he received from various conversations, and he made sure someone was always with me. I was still in shock and denial, sitting on the couch, in the spot where I always sat, waiting for DJ to come home from school or work. At times, the pain was so unbearable I just wanted my heart to stop. I no longer wanted to live. My family and friends stayed very close to me to prevent me from taking my own life. After waiting for about a week, two 18-year-olds turned themselves in to the sheriff's office, but during their line of questioning, they did not offer a lot of information. The sheriff's department followed up on information received from other sources, including information from the interviews of two other people who were being held in connection with the incident. Finally, four people were in jail in connection with DJ's murder, and a year later, a fifth person was arrested. After waiting for an entire year, murder trial preparation began—and so did more waiting.

The police deemed DJ's murder as a "case of mistaken identity." They told us that during their typical investigations into shootings, rarely is there a case of mistaken identity.

Even though it had been more than two years since DJ's death, attending the trials was traumatizing. As I was sitting in the courtroom listening to the details of the night we lost my only child, I was reliving every emotion I experienced that night and every night since that moment. It was hard listening to how they killed my baby in cold blood and then went on with the rest of their night. That did something on the inside of me. I became so hard and cold, and it made me dislike people. When people would say to me, "Oh, you don't mean that," I challenged them by asking, "Have you ever had your only child taken from you? The one you raised to be a decent human being and taught to respect everyone and to do the right thing in life? Until you have lost the light in your life, please don't tell me what I mean!"

I was sitting in court, listening to the details of how my son spent his last moments, and that aspect of the trial shook me to my core. Sometimes, when I am driving at night and realize I am traveling on the same route that led DJ to his death, emotional trauma revisits me. The details I heard throughout the trial play repeatedly in my head as if I were there. Even now, my sense of reality is shaken. I sometimes think and feel DJ should be calling and asking me for money, or asking to borrow my car, or even telling me about some girl that he is interested in. Unfortunately, my phone will never ring with him on the other end. I will never be the person I was when I woke up on the morning of March 5, 2021. DJ's dad and I have endured the trials of those charged with murdering DJ while still on our excruciating journey toward grief recovery. Working through our pain, we continue to give back to the community that embraced us during our time of significant loss.

DJ was a huge Philadelphia Eagles and UGA Bulldog fan. He wore the number 55 in honor of my mom who was born in 1955 and was one of his biggest fans. When he was playing in little league, he wore number 55, and when he began playing sports in high school, he told his coach he wanted to finish his high school football career wearing the same number he started with.

With the funding provided to us through donations, DJ's dad and I started the "Live Like DJ Scholarship Fund" which gives scholarships to high school seniors and first-year college students in the southern region of South Carolina. With the help of a friend, we have also established a "DJ's Day of Giving" which falls on the 55th day of each year (February 24). Each year, on DJ's Day of Giving, local businesses donate a portion of their sales from that day to support our efforts to further endow DJ's scholarship and memorial fund.

Since DJ's death, we have hosted an annual community event to give back to our community who were supportive during our darkest season. "DJ's Day of Giving Back" is held annually during the second weekend in September in celebration of DJ's birthday. This free event includes water slides, games, music, and of course, good food! In addition, we sponsor a 5.5k walk/run that also helps endow DJ's memorial fund which we have set aside to help keep DJ's legacy alive.

Our desire to keep DJ's legacy alive has been well-received within our community. We donate to other local scholarships funds, and we also donate to several charities. Keeping DJ's love for sports in mind, we started a "Live Like DJ Denver Youth Football Scholarship" which helps young people in the Denver, Colorado area. After visiting the Denver area on vacation multiple times, DJ had plans to attend college there. We are honoring him in Denver by starting the scholarship in his name. My sister also lives in Denver, so a piece of him will always be there.

DJ's giving spirit lives on through the donation of turkeys to local sponsored drives during the holidays, and through the toys we buy to be given out to local shelters for kids during Christmas. DJ was the type of person that anyone would have been proud to call their son and although his life was cut short due to senseless gun violence, his dad and I, along with his family and friends, have started "Team 55." Team 55 works effortlessly to continue doing what we know DJ would have loved to do if he were still here.

As we focus on justice for DJ, Team 55 works diligently to ensure that his spirit, love, and legacy help area students achieve their dreams for generations to come. Being able to focus on these initiatives that keep his memory alive is what has given me **my second wind**. The pain of losing my son will never go away, but I can be a beacon of light to others as I honor his memory.

Nikema and DJ

THE JOURNEY BACK TO HER

ANGELA M MITCHELL

There is so much to say, yet there is no need to say it all. I was contemplating telling some long, drawn-out story filled with self-pity and woe is me stories, but, nah. I changed my mind. I'm sharing how I changed the direction of my life quickly and with ease and grace. See, that's the premise, the foundation, the nitty-gritty of it all. Changing my mind was the greatest thing I've done in all the years I've been here, and it's how I got my **second wind**!

Every aspect of my life underwent a transformation—from my self-esteem to relationships, body, spirituality, and business. I decided to stop sitting on the sidelines wallowing in self-pity and get my shit together! It was either that or spend the rest of my life as a fat, miserable, angry mess. The choice was mine, Period!

To say my life has been rough is an understatement, but to describe it as having been all bad is a lie. Yes, I have been a mother and girlfriend since I was seventeen years old and became a grand-mother at thirty-four. I have struggled with my mental health, hard times, and heartache, as many of us have. The thing is, I have always been a survivor and made shit happen for me and mine—no matter what—by any means necessary. That mindset led me to selling drugs, fighting for my life, my children and I being kidnapped at gunpoint, going to jail a few times, fighting a lot, being stabbed twice, committing fraud, and the list goes on. I did what I needed to do to survive over the years to keep a roof over our heads and food on our plates. But I was tired of living in survival mode, you know? I was tired of living check to check and invoice to invoice in my businesses. I was tired of not being heard or appreciated in my relationship and tired of being overweight and full of self-doubt. And really, I was just tired of being tired. One day, I decided enough was enough. That day was January 4, 2020, at 8:00 a.m. Check this out ...

That day started out like any other day. I mean, there I was doing what I usually did at that time in my life, which wasn't much of anything. I was out of work because I messed up my back in 2018, fat as hell because I had gained at least one hundred pounds, my relationship was in shambles, my self-esteem was shot, we were in the middle of a global pandemic, and I was just floating in the wind. The truth is, I had spent the previous four years of my life in a deep depression, feeling sorry for myself, while I was sinking deeper into a darkness that threatened to swallow me whole if I didn't do something to stop it right then! I had allowed depression to become my closest companion, pain became my confidant, and hope felt like an impossible dream that I had long since given up on. But you know what? That day, something inside me shifted.

I was mindlessly scrolling through Facebook, numb and void of any sort of feelings other than the physical and mental exhaustion that came with carrying the weight of my despair, when I ran across a livestream that caught my eye and stopped me dead in my scrolling tracks. The woman on the screen spoke with such conviction that her words pierced through my fog and felt like a lifeline pulling me from the darkness. I had been following her on Facebook for around three years and had watched a few of her videos and reacted to some of her posts, but that day, something was different. As I listened, she was talking directly to me! I caught her on day four of her 31-day devotional series and the topic for that day was about renewing your faith. She had my attention when she talked about how the Most High had already given us everything we needed to get to the other side of our darkest battles. She said, "we are selected, significant, and supplied," and she reminded me that the Most High had chosen me. Her words captivated me as she continued to remind me that I was chosen to serve other women. She said that I am significant, simply because I exist, and I was utterly drawn to her energy. I *knew* we would be connected one day. That woman was Elder Joan T Randall, and she has become my sister, friend, confidant, mentor, and colleague, and I *know* God sent her at just the right time.

Baby, listen—for the first time in who knows how long, I felt something stir inside of me. It was a flicker of hope and a whisper—NO—it was a holler, that maybe, just maybe, it was time to reclaim the woman I'd lost. I had been praying and asking the Most High for an opportunity to be seen, and for the chance to make the dreams I had been holding on to for so long a reality. It was at that moment, with an endless stream of tears running down my face, that I knew I was ready. I was nervous and unsure about my next move, but I knew I had to act, and I did!

I found the courage to inbox her that day to let her know how much of an impact her words had on me. Whew! Little did I know how that single act of swallowing my fear and sending her that message would be instrumental in leading me back to *her*—back to the fierce, feminine, fearless, and faith-filled woman I was sent here to be.

The assignment was to take out my journal and write what I loved most about myself. I struggled to come up with an answer, but I said that I loved my heart and the love I gave to others. After doing that initial exercise, and the ones that followed, I couldn't get enough of writing in my journal. I wanted to write all the time! Going through those thirty-one days of self-reflection and devotion was exactly what I needed to help me along the journey to healing I had started a few months prior.

I know for a fact that God sends who you need when you are ready to receive it, and not a second before. I had been praying and asking for years for the opportunity to be seen. I have been wanting to write and tap into the online space for years and I was ready to move from the sidelines. Growing my faith and trusting that God was waiting for me to see myself was the motivation that got me to the other side of the darkness I had existed in for so long. And yes, I merely existed because there is no life where there is no hope. Finally, I recognized and accepted that I had been struggling with my mental health for many years, so I got the help I needed to stop repeating the same cycle. I was diagnosed with Bipolar II disorder, and generalized anxiety disorder, but the best part was that I finally had a name for the thing that had plagued me my whole life. I was so thankful to finally understand the extreme depressive lows and crazy manic highs I had been going through.

People make light of depression and bipolar disorder, and I used to do that until I really understood what it was and how it had been affecting my ability to function. I would go weeks, and sometimes months, so depressed that I was literally operating on autopilot. There were days that I could not get up and when I did, my mood was foul, or I would be distant. Then, there were the manic highs where I had more energy than I knew what to do with, and that had me creating and starting things I would never finish. I had to get my mind right, so even though I wasn't completely convinced it would work, I started medication. The next thing I did after my diagnosis was center and ground myself spiritually. There was no way I was getting to the next level without it, so I reconnected with Source so that I could be present and completely self-aware. I distanced myself from low vibrating energy, activities, and people, which of course had people looking at me crazy and telling me I was acting funny. No, I was not acting funny, I was getting in tune with my emotional, physical, and spiritual self, and positioning myself to listen so I could hear God! I had so much inside, so much that had been lying dormant just waiting for the chance to pop out and shine through, and nothing or no one was going to stop me again!

Over the next few months, I set out to navigate my way in the world of writing and online entrepreneurship. Yes, I had been an entrepreneur since 2012, when I launched my first blog, but this was different. This time, the stakes were higher, and I was fighting for my life! I joined a writing challenge, which led to me becoming a co-author in my first anthology, "The Image in the Mirror." In my chapter, "She Needed a Hero," I shared things I had never shared with anyone before. I finally got shit off my chest that I had been holding on to for decades. My journey to reinvention had begun.

I Changed the Narrative

The first and most important step to take when you are ready to level up is to change your mind. There really is no other way. Negative and self-limiting beliefs stop you in your tracks and keep you from realizing how powerful you are, and that's what happened to me. When I looked back at the experiences and challenges, I faced, I noticed a pattern of self-doubt and insecurity. I recognized that each hurdle, every heartbreak or negative thing, started with a decision resulting from a poisonous thought. Honestly, I had thought myself into poverty, bad relationships, and a stagnant, unfulfilling life. I convinced myself that I couldn't start a successful business and live the life I always dreamed of, so I settled for mediocrity and slowly died on the inside.

Man, it's hard to look at yourself in the mirror and admit that *you* are the issue in your life and that your problems are not anyone else's fault. It's even harder when you are heading towards fifty years old and realize just how much of your life you gave to others compared to how little you invested in yourself. Yes, it was time for me to dig in and look into my eyes, but I hated the image of brokenness looking back at me. I was so busy blaming other folks for the things that happened to me, I forgot I was the only one who had the power to decide how I respond to life. That's the power of self-awareness, and that's when my mindset transformation began.

I addressed every area of my life. Finances, love life, business, relationships, *ALL* of it. I took everyone else out of the equation and finally saw that my thoughts led to an action (or inaction), and the action led to a result, and they were not the results I wanted. Instead of focusing on what I didn't want, I turned my full attention to what I *did* want, and I stopped making excuses. I created an action list of what it would take to achieve my goals, made a plan, and got busy doing what I needed to do. For a while, I was stuck being a perpetual student. I took a lot of courses and became certified in everything from mindset to marketing. I had the knowledge and experience, but I wasn't taking the actions needed to go beyond coaching folks for free. The problem was that those beliefs started to creep in and show up as fear of success, fear of being seen, and being scared of doing something different.

I used to worry about what my friends and family would think about me changing and taking my life in a new and better direction. I feared being visible and not being accepted because I didn't believe in myself, but I was determined not to let any more time go by without me creating a legacy for my children and my children's children. When I changed all those ridiculous beliefs and moved beyond them, I released all my negative energy around money and set myself in a position where I could make more of it without shame, guilt, or anxious feelings. I can't believe I used to think I wasn't deserving of more, and I would never get it anyway. The best part of it was I finally gained the confidence to ask for what I wanted, and I was no longer afraid to go get it.

My Second Wind

I am a firm believer that clarity breeds peace and confidence, and when you remember who you are and what you came here to do, abundance will flow to you easily. I am at that point in my life where I know who I am, whose I am, and what I want out of the rest of my days. When I tell you that everything I prayed about, wrote in my journal, and daydreamed about are coming to pass, it's to let you know that it can happen for you too! All it takes is one more action to get there. I never thought I would be an author of several books, serving as Director of Marketing for Victorious You Press, speaking to women all over the world, and hosting interviews on my own show in less than four years. But God!

Getting clear was a huge deal for me because there was a time when I was so fearful of rejection that when I received feedback that didn't align with what I thought they needed, it felt like a personal attack. I would get upset and retreat like a baby having a tantrum and miss out on growth opportunities, but, when I took the time to be still and listen to God's whispers, I understood how deep those lies went and how powerful my mind was.

I became the woman I visualized, the teacher, the author, the coach, the college graduate, the homeowner, the speaker, and the CEO. I walked, talked, and operated daily as the person I wanted to be, but, first, I had to transform my thoughts, actions, and behaviors. I stopped fighting, stopped resisting, and, most importantly, eliminated the disobedience and embraced my purpose. Every goal I have accomplished over the past four years is the result of God's grace and mercy. All those visions were previews of what was to come, and it all has come to pass! It was always there, just waiting for *me* to catch up. I got a second chance! I got **my second wind**, baby, and I am never looking back!

IT'S HELL IN THE HALLWAY

KRISTY BUSIJA

O n the day I jumped on a virtual meeting call with my manager for my annual performance review, I noticed something unusual. Usually, only my manager would appear, but on that particular day, it was my manager, the Human Resources manager, and the Vice President of Human Resources on the call. My heart immediately sank, my chest tightened, and I could feel the blood draining from my body. My mind started racing, frantically trying to grasp what could be the reason for all of them showing up for my review. In my 20-plus years as part of the HR team, the only time there were that many people appearing on a call was when there was bad news to be delivered, and witnesses were needed. The conversation that ensued caused my mind to go blank momentarily. Then, came the words that changed everything: "We're letting you go for not living the company values. We've coached you about this several times and haven't seen any changes."

Whatever was said after that was lost for all eternity. You could have knocked me over with a feather! Up until that very moment, I had received stellar reviews, and I was listed as my manager's successor. All I could hear were my thoughts which were racing at 1,000 miles a minute. My mind was scrambling to recall any conversation we may have had about what I was being accused of. I was frantically trying to remember any coaching moment, or any feedback I had received concerning the matter they were presenting, while my chest grew tighter, and my head started pounding. My mind drew a complete blank because those conversations never happened! I asked for specific examples, to which they said: "We're not providing you with any of that information." After the shock wore off my mind continued to race, but in another direction.

What will happen to my benefits? How will I pay my mortgage and bills? I felt helpless and was taken back to the previous two companies (yes, two!) and the conversations which were held when I was told my role was being eliminated because of a reorganization. *What in the world? How can this be happening again? And what is this garbage about not living the values?!* The ping-pong of thoughts and emotions made me dizzy, and I felt out of control. Then, like a light switch being flipped on, resolve and determination kicked in. My mind came to a screeching halt, my focus sharpened, and the blood started to rise. Suddenly, my emotions took a turn to anger. I was angry about the name bubbles that appeared on the screen. How could they deliver a message like that and not at least turn on the cameras and look me in the eye. I was angry at the company for fabricating conversations that never happened and for attacking my character. I was angry at my leader for also lying about having conversations that never happened!

The anger that arose was swiftly replaced by a strong resolve—a firm determination. One door had violently shut in my face, and I found myself in the hallway between two doors. One door had just slammed closed behind me and the thing that represented my purpose and destiny seemed to be hidden behind one of the seemingly endless doors at the end of the hallway. There were no other open doors, and I certainly couldn't go back. I was stuck in the hallway.

If you've ever been in a hallway, you know that it's cold, damp, and so dark that you can't see far ahead. Sure, there is a tiny sliver of light up ahead, but the farther you walk, the farther away it seems! There is no one else in the hallway with you because it is *your* journey to traverse and navigate. There are a few supporters who peek through the tiny windows every once in a while, but it is truly your path to take, not theirs.

As I moved away from the closed door, I tried every door to my left and right. Each one was firmly locked, but unlike my last hallway experiences, I felt a fire inside of me. Instead of tentatively walking down that hallway and frantically trying every door I encountered, I put one foot in front of the other and started to run. I was running away from what had been holding me back for more than 23 years and running toward my future. I was running toward the door that opened to the passion that God planted inside me. Even though the sliver of light ahead looked so far off, I found myself running toward the next door and the next door and the next door, because I innately knew that the right door would open. I knew I would reach the door that I could walk through to live out my purpose and passion for helping people feel valued, heard, respected, and seen. People always say that when one door closes, another one opens, but what they don't tell you is--"It's HELL in the hallway!"

My career has been a beautiful tapestry of breaking down barriers, infusing ways to get to the heartbeat of an organization and finding ways to create environments where people can be motivated to take action. I am known, rewarded, and celebrated for doing what others can't do and for making sense of what seems like chaos. At one organization, instead of just reporting numbers and beating leaders over the head with how they were not meeting expectations, I leaned in with them to create a monthly dashboard. They had full authority over every aspect of it, from what it looked like to the information included, the discussion approach, accountability, and what they needed in the way of support. As it rolled out, what I saw was somewhat of a miracle.

The numbers started climbing and the conversations were happening; so much so, that our region surpassed every other region. We became the benchmark for the organization and were asked to share our scorecard and best practices with the other regions. Leaders were no longer acting out of pure compliance but were taking action because they understood the value of what they were doing and wanted to make a difference. The information only confirmed the benefits of all their hard work in doing what was right and developing their employees. I brought all of what I do best to that pivotal organization.

Fast forward a couple of years to the very organization that would eventually start me on my true path. Talent conversations were seen as a nuisance, a painful conversation. Even the CEO commented that he saw no value because there was never any movement (that he could see). Challenge accepted. I got to work. I looked closely at every conversation throughout the year and dove head-first into the data. The value of something cannot be determined if there is no visibility, measurement, or observation of its impact. Out popped another collaborative dashboard, highlighting the "now" and showcasing what we aspired to achieve. I was equipping the leaders on *how to* have the conversations, *how* to shift their mindset, etc. We held leadership team calls and rallied around the leaders, teaching them how to create development plans, how to encourage one another, and how to provide support.

As our leaders were learning how to be vulnerable, transparent, and supportive, we started to see the sea of red turn yellow, then green. In less than a year, the organization had surpassed the goal we initially set forth and we were looking to what was next. At that organization, I was tasked with revamping succession planning to showcase the abilities of employees at all levels, not just those favored by top executives. I revolutionized conversations between managers and employees and shifted them from being purely transactional to being intentional and purposeful. I brought in best-in-class training programs to empower leaders to lead transformationally, resulting in $2 million in savings through strategic partnerships and enterprise strategy alignment. I was applauded for my contributions and was subsequently listed to be my leader's successor.

Looking back, perhaps things went south for me because I kept telling the wrong person "No" too many times. I refused to bend on my ethics and morals, particularly when it came to doing right by the employees. One of my largest contributions was the introduction of a holistic assessment strategy, to ensure we hired the right people for the right roles and then developed them to maximize their purpose and potential. Everything from personality assessments (who you are) to 360-degree feedback (how others perceive you). I spent painstaking hours partnering closely with our legal counsel (United States and European Union), and the HR business partners to ensure that the information we were gathering from our employees would remain confidential and would be used for good and not evil. That was also the message that was communicated to each employee. I labored over who would see information and how it would or wouldn't be used, but out of the blue, the VP of HR asked me to begin sending assessment reports directly to managers and herself.

I consistently pointed the leadership back to what we had agreed upon and had communicated to the employees. When she asked again, I directed her back to what we communicated and committed to our employees. Apparently, that wasn't what she wanted to hear.

One day, her request that I surrender the employee information turned into a demand.

"The company paid for the assessment and the data belongs to the company. Give it to me and the manager," she demanded.

Thought bubbles popped up that were not very professional, so as diplomatically as I could muster, I walked her through the process to make that happen. I educated her on GDPR law and the ethics of sharing data without the knowledge of the employee. For those not familiar, GDPR is the General Data Protection Regulation, a European Union (EU) law that regulates how personal data is used and is considered one of the world's strictest data protection and privacy laws. (Violation of GDPR law doesn't end well, in case you are wondering). I pleaded my case with her, on behalf of the employees who were assured that their information would be safe, that surrendering their information would erode trust with employees. After months of back and forth, I was fired for "not living the company values." To this day, I still don't know which of the company values I did not live up to. Was it integrity? Respect? Accountability? All I know for sure is that I held to my ethical moral compass and my values, despite being continually asked to violate the trust of the people we vowed to protect.

After three years, and a ton of self-reflection, coaching, and therapy, I've realized a few things. Perhaps the most obvious lesson I learned is to only align myself with organizations that share my conviction and commitment to doing the right thing and acting with integrity and transparency. The more profound thing I realized, which has fueled me ever since that fateful day, is that God was slamming a door on something that wasn't aligned with my purpose; namely, my deep-seated passion to help people feel valued, heard, seen, and respected. In fact, He was handing me my running shoes, helping me lace them up, and holding up a lamp in front of me to guide me through the dark and damp hallway. That sliver of light that kept moving further away wasn't to taunt or discourage me, it was to light my way and show me the next step and the direction to take to truly live out my calling and use my God-given gifts. All I had to do was keep taking steps, keep running the race, and persevere.

That day was the day when I, with full confidence and determination, moved from being on the treadmill that others defined for me, and where they controlled my steps and fate. That was the day I started running *my* race in *my* way. My business (my side hustle) was a side hustle no more! I made a choice that, no matter what would come my way, my business was going to thrive and flourish, and I have not looked back since! I will, without question, help organizations create environments where employees feel valued, heard, respected, and seen. Period.

Looking back over my journey, I realize that all the things I experienced, the things I have done, and the people I have encountered, have given me a unique perspective and amazing insight into how to treat people as humans. My experience has taught me how to truly hear what they want and need in order to unlock their purpose and passion. Heck, even the worst experiences have been fertile training grounds, even if just to show me what *not* to do. The workplace bullying I encountered at the hand of employees, the slander that was spread about me, the two back-to-back reductions in force (layoffs), and even the colleagues that decided it was their mission to sabotage me, all revealed to me the fragility of the human condition and how important it is to protect not just the bottom line, but the people who are doing the work and making a difference. To paraphrase one of my favorite humans, my coach, my friend, Colin Callahan, "It's not my forever, it's just my for now."

Keep moving ahead, embrace the learning along the way, and lean into the journey. Your door will open, the path you should take will become clearer, and what an amazing adventure it will be! When I embraced the hallway, I got **my second wind**, and it has fueled me to keep running!

PURPOSE DEFIES AGE

CHARMAINE LAFONDÉ

Have you ever felt empty after investing so much in other people's lives and neglecting your own? Entering my sixtieth decade, I began seriously thinking, *"How am I going to spend the rest of my life?"* My adult children were living their lives, and I was living with regret for what I considered to be so many wasted years. Years into my fourth marriage, I was unsatisfied with my life, and I did not want my future to be more of the same. I was tired of pretending to have it all together on the outside, knowing I felt like a failure.

The idea of not accomplishing my life's purpose made me anxious, and death started to feel like a welcome relief. I kept asking myself, *"If money and time were not an obstacle, how would I want to spend my last days on earth?"* I felt the clock ticking. It dawned on me that I was feeling so unfulfilled because I was living my life out of alignment with God's perfect plan. On August 21, 2017, everything changed. On that day, I found out on Facebook that my 32-year-old son, Curtis, was dead.

I was on my lunch break at work when my daughter called to inform me about disturbing Facebook posts she had encountered. I cut my lunch short to go to my desk to investigate. I scrolled through the posts in disbelief. I could feel my heartbeat bouncing off my chest cavity and reverberating in my ears like a drum. *"No, this can't be* true," I thought. I kept scrolling, looking for any indication that the R.I.P.s were a very cruel joke. I maintained my composure and calmly searched my mind for the next course of action. I decided to dial my son's number because I thought, *"If he sees that it's me calling, he will pick up."* With each ring, I was hoping to hear his typical loud and obnoxious greeting: " Heyyyyyy Mommaaaaaaa!" No answer. I paused for a moment, then dialed again. I was relieved that someone answered, but it was not Curtis' voice on the other end.

"Who is this?" I asked. The person who answered identified himself as a friend of my son. My next question to him was very direct: *"What happened to Curtis?"* In an almost incoherent manner, with a noticeable and rambling stutter, he gave me his rendition of what happened to my son. He told me about what happened after finding my son's lifeless body, and then he gave me the phone number of the NYPD detective who was handling my son's case. After that conversation, I calmly hung up the phone.

I grabbed the notepad on which I had written the detective's phone number and a pen and then slowly and deliberately headed towards a conference room to make my next call in a more private space. With each step towards the conference room, I could feel something about to come up from the depths of my belly. I tried to contain it until I reached the conference room and closed the door, but I didn't get that far. I reached the staircase next to the conference room and let out a wail I could no longer contain. It was a sound of anguish that one of my co-workers must have recognized. She was heard saying, "Someone has just lost a child."

The course of my future was established in that pivotal moment. I had reached my lowest point and was a prime candidate to have my life restored from the ground up. Three pillars were established in my heart that day, and my future life would be built upon them.

1. **Listen intently to the voice of God for his instructions**. He will lead and guide me every step of the way. When I finally made it into that conference room, still wailing at the very top of my lungs, God spoke to me clear as a bell. What he said caused my tears to dry up *immediately!*

2. **God himself is peace.** After he spoke three sobering words to me, I felt an overwhelming peace. Have you ever heard of a peace that passes understanding? I experienced that.

3. **Forgive.** In that moment of overwhelming peace and calm, I forgave everyone involved in any way with my son's death. I didn't have any details about what happened, but I knew forgiveness had to take place. Unforgiveness leads to a root of bitterness, which blocks blessings and makes life miserable.

From that moment, God began instructing me, and his voice was crystal clear. *"Pay attention to what is happening; you'll have to write about it."* My grief journey had begun, and you best believe, I needed to hear his voice like never before. I was in unchartered waters.

That afternoon, after my initial conversation with the NYPD, I was livid! I spoke with a detective who was cold in his response to my inquiries. He promised to call back with any updates, but he did not ask for my name or phone number. When I hung up the phone, I could feel a fire within which was about to burst into a flaming inferno. I quickly looked for something to hurl across the room when I heard God's firm voice. *"Be angry, but sin not."* One of the key elements that helped me to navigate the days, weeks, months and years which were to come was my ability to recognize God's voice. God is always speaking; the question is, are we listening?

"The gatekeeper opens the gate for him, and the sheep listen to his voice. He calls his own sheep by name and leads them out. When he has brought out all his own, he goes on ahead of them, and his sheep follow him because they know his voice. But they will never follow a stranger; in fact, they will run away from him because they do not recognize a stranger's voice. John 10:3-5 (NIV)

When Curtis died, I vowed to "live my life to the fullest." God was revealing the blueprint for how I could do just that, and he had my FULL attention!

Supernatural occurrences were not weird to me, as I was very familiar with how God operates outside of the natural realm. I wanted to live the rest of my life with the overwhelming peace that filled my heart and the room where I was sitting on that fateful day.

Little did I know that God's plan for my future included me walking out the rest of my days in peace. As He walked with me through the valley of the shadow of Curtis' death, I contended to hold onto peace. The blueprint for holding onto peace included instructions on how I could do it. I began by identifying the things in my life that were draining my peace. I identified the obstacles blocking my peace, and very intentionally, I began to address and eliminate them from my life. I was making room for the things I wanted to allow in my life by getting rid of what no longer served me.

I did not have a clear picture of what my future would look like, but I knew God had a plan for my life. Taking a step of faith, I formed a company, *The LaFondé Experience,* and shortly after that, I became a published author. I published my first book at the age of 62. *"Who Killed My Son? A Mother's Wait for Justice"* was just the beginning of my writing career. God has a way of turning things around to work for our good. Becoming an author opened a portal to more writing opportunities. I began writing encouraging messages as a ray of hope for those who had encountered the darkness that accompanies grief. Who would have thought that the death of my child would lead to a life of purpose? God knew.

"For I know the plans I have for you," declares the Lord, "plans to prosper you and not to harm you, plans to give you hope and a future." Jeremiah 29:11

While God was doing his part by keeping his promises to me, I was doing my part by cooperating with him. I was cultivating an attitude of gratitude. Things may not always be the way we want them to be in life, but rather than being bitter or disgruntled, try a little gratitude. We often don't appreciate what we have until it's gone. Even though my son was no longer with me, I took a solemn look at what remained. Do you ever find yourself complaining so much about what is wrong or missing that you neglect to count your blessings? When I stopped looking back on my past with regret and began to have a different perspective on what was ahead, more opportunities unfolded right before my eyes! My perspective cleared away the dark cloud that had overshadowed my future, and suddenly, things began to appear brighter. What was once a dark tunnel of grief and hopelessness, gave way to hope and potential. I took radical steps to preserve not only the peace that was becoming an integral part of my being but the guiding light that was leading me to prosperity in other areas of my life! My faith was getting stronger.

Taking a deeper look within me revealed that other giants were still occupying space in my soul. I did not want to take them into my future, and I was ready to face them. I did not want them to impede my growth any longer; I had a race to run and did not want to be hindered. I had been held captive long enough. I set out to slay those giants I could readily identify upon self-reflection and called them out to be dealt with. Past trauma, insecurities, fear, rejection, disappointment, a mindset contrary to what God was saying to me in that season, and any form of unforgiveness that remained in my heart. Unforgiveness was the most deadly of them all.

For the first time in decades, I began to experience a satisfaction in life that I had not previously enjoyed. I was becoming a better, more authentic version of me! I began decluttering decades of junk which had accumulated over years, and I felt much lighter. I was connected to a local church and really appreciated the "faith partners" that I formed a relationship with. By the time I published my fifth book, I was living and fulfilling one of my deepest desires—helping others.

I have always had a heart to serve, but I began to cultivate a deeper sense of helping others by sharing my story and helping them to share theirs. I incorporated freelance editing into my business and started serving writers who wanted help writing their stories. I was evolving as a businesswoman, something I never saw in my future. God was steadily guiding me into that beautiful future he promised.

Six years had passed since my son's death, and I found myself still waiting for some type of justice concerning his case. The assailant, who is known to the NYPD, has yet to be arrested. I thought again about the supernatural encounter I had with God in that conference room. I reflected, time and time again, on the moment when I forgave everyone involved with his death. I understood how unforgiveness blocks blessings, and I didn't want that to be a part of my future.

"But if you don't forgive others, then your Father in heaven will not forgive the wrongs you do." Matthew 6:15 (ERV)

I did not want my breakthrough to be hindered, so I looked deep into my heart for any trace of unforgiveness. *"If I can forgive everyone responsible for my son's death, I can forgive ANYBODY!"* I told myself. Then, I caught a reflection in the mirror of the one person I had not forgiven for the devastation in my life. That was quite the "aha moment!" I did the difficult task of forgiving myself for my past failures and accepted God's forgiveness. That was a setup for a miracle!

On August 21, 2023, exactly six years from the day I learned of Curtis' death, I received my complete heart healing, and grief left my life! I sat alone in my prayer closet and invited the pain of his death to come. When I realized that there were no more triggers (random thoughts that would cause tears to flow) and no more sadness when I thought about my son, I embraced the healing of my heart and considered my grief journey to be over. I will always bear the scar, but the pain, the triggers, and the sadness associated with his death have been completely eradicated from my life! God turned it around for good!!

I couldn't have even fathomed the life I am living now when I was thinking about retirement just a few years earlier. I am living a fulfilled life, doing the things I enjoy with the people I enjoy doing life with. The mask-wearing impostor has been replaced by a cleansed and free new me! Showing up as my authentic self is all the more reason for me to smile! God had a plan for my life all along, but I needed to come into agreement with allowing him to bring his original plan to manifestation in my life. I learned that listening intently to his voice and doing things his way leads to rewards without regret or sorrow. I also learned that I was worthy of forgiveness, no matter how bad I may have messed up in the past. The most important person in the world that I needed to forgive was myself. I have.

Be encouraged! If you are still breathing, God's plan of redemption is available and is yours for the asking. My son's death had me questioning everything I had ever known or believed about the goodness of God, but he has proven his faithfulness to me. It takes courage to trust God, but the more you get to know him, the easier it is.

God has given me a NEW song to sing–it is the song of the redeemed. He has given me **my second wind,** restored the joy of my salvation and turned my mourning into dancing again! I have found my calling and am living my dreams.

God is well aware of what time it is, so if you feel it is too late for you to have all that he promised, step away from being controlled by your emotions—they lie, but God's word does not.

DROWNING IN MY PLACE OF COMFORT

CHRISTAL SPENCE NEWKIRK

"For God did not give us a spirit of timidity or cowardice or fear, but [He has given us a spirit] of power and of love and of sound judgment and personal discipline [abilities that result in a calm, well-balanced mind and self-control]". 2 Timothy 1:7 (Amplified)

Have you ever felt stuck in a corporate position with no growth potential, or stuck in an unfaithful marriage? Do you know what it's like to be stuck in a business with no profits, or stuck in an unhealthy relationship or friendship? Well, you are not alone. For years, my 9-to-5 job was my comfort zone and my hiding place. While I developed many talents, my God-given gifts remained hidden, leaving me feeling unfulfilled. I knew God was directing me to trust Him and take a faith step toward my entrepreneurial passion, but I was stuck in comfort and fear. When I prayed and searched my heart to understand the root of my fear, I realized it was connected to my childhood.

43

Growing up with a single parent of seven children, I was familiar with humble beginnings. My mom did her best to provide for our family. I am forever thankful that my mom did not abandon us or give us away. Because of that, she is my forever shero. My grit, determination and strong business acumen came from my mom and watching how she handled life's challenges. However, as the oldest daughter, I was always aware of our financial struggle. My childhood experiences played a major role in my adult decisions. As the oldest daughter, I picked up the burden of worry, fear and anxiety at a very young age. The fear of experiencing lack again kept me stuck in my comfort zone in my adult life. Because of that, I worked more hours weekly than the average person. I wanted to have extra savings to help my family and those that were in need. Even though the burden was heavy, I did not share it with anyone, nor did I ask for help, and as a result I felt the overwhelming water levels of life as I was treading daily to stay afloat for years. Some days, it felt like I was submerged mentally and emotionally, and at one point, my physical health was greatly impacted.

On May 1, 2023, I woke up around 4:25 a.m. having difficulty breathing. I immediately walked downstairs to share my symptoms and discomfort with my husband, who typically left for work around 5:00 a.m. He checked my blood pressure, gave me an aspirin, but when I felt no relief after fifteen minutes, he rushed me to the hospital. After running several tests, the ER doctor informed us that there were multiple blood clots in my lungs. Thirty days prior, I had a minor procedure performed, but due to my lack of movement during recovery, the blood clots formed. Typically, I exercise three or four times weekly, but because of my heavy workload, I was extremely tired mentally and overwhelmed emotionally. After that health scare, I knew I needed to make some lifestyle changes and, more importantly, I knew I needed to surrender to God.

For over a year, I prayed for courage and confidence to take the faith step to leave my full-time job and step into the next level of purpose. I believed that Jesus Christ was my Jehovah Jireh, according to Philippians 4:19, but I was still very hesitant to obey His instructions. God's word states that obedience is better than sacrifice, but as you know, we obey those that we trust. The real question was "Did I trust God enough to surrender to His plan and purpose?" While reviewing my emotional intelligence assessment results, my executive coach, Lisa Medley, asked me "In the face of uncertainty, do you trust that you have the ability to find the solution? How do you build trust? What do you need to feel safe?"

REFLECTION QUESTION: I was challenged in the area of trusting God enough to step into full-time entrepreneurship. In which area in your life do you feel you need more trust? What do you need to feel confident enough to move out of your comfort zone?

Taking a Faith Step

On June 27, 2024, I showed up at my job to coordinate an onsite hiring event. My favorite manager was on leave for a few months, so I reported to an interim manager. While speaking to my interim manager, I was reminded of a warning-type dream God showed me a few months prior. The dream had an unfavorable ending which indicated that if I continued to work past a certain day, it would cost me greatly.

After that conversation with my interim manager, I rushed home, my heart racing. I knew that day was a pivotal moment. Would I obey God? Once I arrived at home, I received an email from my interim manager that confirmed it was time for me to leave. Her micro-management style did not align with my personality. I always knew if I ever had to work for her that I would leave that position. After reading her email, I immediately turned in my two-weeks' notice. After I sent that email, the water levels of my life began to recede and I felt the overwhelming emotional pressure I had been sensing lifted. I cried a cry of relief, then I called my husband to let him know what I had done. I had been talking to him about leaving that position for over a year, so I was excited that I finally committed to taking action. I know my determination to achieve something greater in life came from my faith in God's word and my spiritual relationship, and I believed God had a better future planned for my life. If you truly have faith and believe God's word, then you must take action. True faith requires corresponding action.

REFLECTION QUESTION: Can you think of a time when you desired more out of your life, but you felt stuck in comfort? What motivated you to take action? Or, what do you need now to help you to take action today?

Saying YES to God

In December 2021, I said yes to God to expand my business and obtain my diverse supplier certifications. The process was frustrating, and the journey was a very lonely one. I did not know anyone else that was seriously pursuing government contracting, so I prayed to God for help. During the summer of 2022, I decided to hire a mentor who I had been following online since the pandemic. Joining the "Power Play" mentoring program, with my mentor, Denise Taylor, was one of the best investments for my business, my personal health, and my marriage. Through that investment, I was able to obtain clarity, develop confidence, and implement an intentional self-care routine. I knew I needed to make lifestyle changes, but I did not think there would be a two-year delay before I took action. Part of the delay was due to my lack of courage and confidence to leave my safety net. Even though I believed God had more planned for my life, when I looked in the mirror, I saw the little girl that did not feel safe or confident. For years, I meditated on Ephesians 2:10 to develop courage and confidence to take the next faith step to become a full-time entrepreneur.

"For we are His workmanship [His own master work, a work of art], created in Christ Jesus [reborn from above—spiritually transformed, renewed, ready to be used] for good works, which God prepared [for us] beforehand [taking paths which He set], so that we would walk in them [living the good life which He prearranged and made ready for us]." Ephesians 2:10 (Amplified).

This scripture really resonates with me because I believe everyone is designed with specific gifts and talents that make them a special, one-of-a-kind individual. Based upon our unique design, I believe there is a right path that has been preplanned for us to walk to complete our purpose, impact lives, and enjoy the good life that has been made available for us.

In the spirit of transparency, I was afraid to surrender to God and leave my full-time position even though God had already proven He would abundantly provide for me and my family as I worked full-time as an entrepreneur. I understood that surrender meant I had to agree to stop fighting, resisting and hiding from God. During my 20 years as a full-time employee, my God-given gifts remained untapped, which deeply affected my self-confidence and sense of purpose. I knew there was more to life for me, and I felt God calling me to step into a purpose far greater than I had imagined, one that would transform my life and the lives of others.

In December 2023, God revealed to me in a dream that I would be on a stage speaking in front of a large audience. I immediately thought the dream was from the devil because I was not a public speaker. I enjoyed coaching and empowering individuals on a 1:1 or small group basis, but I never thought of myself as a public speaker. When I had the same dream again, I knew it was God. I said "yes," and thanks to my purpose-pusher friend, LaVada Humphrey, who encouraged me to obey God, I registered for a Toastmaster's class. See, when God gives me a new assignment, He always brings the right people into my life to assist me in fulfilling the assignment. On the flip side, God also revealed friendships that had expired and no longer fit in the inner circle of my life. For every new season and new assignment, I am learning how to develop and embrace the new gift as well as remove friendships that do not align with God's instructions. I've also learned that, in every new season, I need to give myself grace and space to learn and become.

REFLECTION QUESTIONS: Has God revealed any new gift(s) that He wants to use in the current season of your life? Is there a new area in your life that you need to give yourself grace and space so that you can learn and become what God has called you to do? What do you need in this new season?

Embracing New Beginnings

In December 2023, I said yes to an opportunity to purchase a Queen City Women in Business franchise for the state of Georgia. Even though I prayed for years about expanding my business, I never imagined purchasing a franchise. The reason I said yes to the opportunity was because I prayed and discussed it with my husband first. Secondly, I experienced great peace because I knew the decision aligned with my passion, purpose, and my business goal to expand my business. In May 2024, I signed the contract and purchased the QCWIB-Georgia license for one year. God revealed that it was a short-term assignment that would have a long-term impact. Because of my obedience, I've been able to successfully impact my family, friends and community, providing training on how to expand their business, obtain diverse supplier certification, create another stream of income, and build legacy wealth.

My husband and I discovered that his 30+ years of construction experience was in very high demand as a diverse supplier, so he joined our family business part-time as the Vice President of our new Construction Staffing, Safety and Facilities Maintenance

Services Division. This is the third business venture that my husband and I have worked on together. Each business venture was training and preparation for the next one, and we are excited to see what God will do through us, for us and with us.

On Friday, July 12, 2024, I turned in my laptop and home-office equipment to my employer and fully embraced my new role as a full-time entrepreneur, entering into the next level of my purpose. That day represented a new beginning and **a second wind for me**.

It took a few years for me to develop courage and confidence to surrender to God and embrace my entrepreneurial passion. Below are five steps that helped me to embrace courage and walk confidently and powerfully in the next level of my purpose.

1. My first step was to identify and defeat the root cause that was hindering my progress. That was not an overnight process, but an intentional journey that included me seeking professional help. I've worked on my fear issues with a professional counselor for years.

2. My second step was to overcome the imposter syndrome and self-limiting beliefs through spiritual growth. My Elevation e-group family supported me in my spiritual journey. We read books and shared our challenges with accountability, support, prayer and love.

3. My third step involved implementing a self-care routine that supported my new demands. Intentional self-care has helped improve my overall mental health by reducing stress and anxiety. It has also helped with my spiritual

relationship as well as my emotional and physical health. To achieve the full benefit of an effective self-care program, it was important that I block off my calendar on a daily, weekly, monthly, or quarterly basis to focus on self-care and quality alone time.

4. My fourth step was to invest in a mentor or coach. For every major change or new assignment in my life, I've invested in a mentor or coach to walk with me on that particular leg of my journey. There are no new tricks that Satan can use to try to stop me from walking in purpose and living the good life that God has already prepared for me. Fear and self-doubt always appear when it is time for me to move out of my comfort zone; therefore, we are not called to walk this journey alone. I believe God has the right help available for every assignment and transition He has called me to.

5. My fifth step included praying, and selecting the right community of like-minded, Christian women who have the same goals and assigned to walk with me in this season. The people in my inner circle are a cornerstone of my life. I love the lyrics to a song by Ne-Yo (Make Me Better). "I am a movement by myself. But I am a force when we are together." I believe women small business owners can accomplish more through the right collaboration and strategic partnership.

REFLECTION QUESTIONS: Which of the above steps resonates with you the most? What is stopping you from living the best life God prepared for you? What help do you need?

With the decline of our current economy and new administration, many people feel discouraged, overwhelmed, stuck and fearful. My journey from corporate to my entrepreneurial calling is about finding the courage and confidence to rise above fear, tap into the power within, and claim the life I was meant to live. My hope is to inspire anyone who feels stuck, lost, discouraged and unsure of their next step. I give you permission today to stop hiding, fighting and resisting God. Trust God and surrender to His Plan for your life. Find your tribe and don't walk this journey alone. Focus on one step at a time and take the next step!

FINALLY FREE TO FIND ME

SHARON R THOMPSON

I was too young to understand where we were headed. In my youthful mind, it was just another routine car ride with my mother. As we drove down the road, my mother suddenly stopped when she spotted my brother. What happened next set in motion the beginning of the childhood trauma I would come to know.

The moment my brother saw my mother's car, he ran! Leaving me behind, my mother jumped out of the car and ran in the direction my brother had taken. Apparently, my mother found my brother hiding in the bushes and shot him. After I heard the gunshot, I heard my mother say, "You will learn not to steal from me!"

I was shocked at what I had just witnessed and sat helplessly in the car. My mother helped my bleeding brother walk to the car, then helped him to get in. There was blood flowing from somewhere on his body, but I could not tell where he had been shot. I knew better than to say anything, so I sat quietly trying to process what was happening and why. My brother was crying in pain and I wanted to comfort him, but I did not know how. I just remember being so scared for him and wondering, "*What did he steal to make her so mad?*" I had no idea what was going to happen next, so I sat quietly as my mother drove to our next destination.

When the car stopped, we were at the police station. We went inside where my mother almost proudly announced that she had shot my brother, and they needed to get him some help. She sat there as though nothing had happened while the police called for an ambulance to transport my brother to the hospital. To this day, I still don't know if my mother was ever charged for shooting my brother.

As I reminisce over my life, there were so many traumatic childhood experiences that negatively impacted me. I clearly recalled when I was eleven years old, being overwhelmed by the humiliation I felt being teased by my classmates. No one had prepared me with the essential knowledge about self-care during my menstrual cycle. I was not taught to wear deodorant either, so I didn't understand why I was being singled out and teased. One day, to avoid being teased, I decided to skip school. That day, my stepfather gave me guidance on personal hygiene. He introduced me to deodorant and personal care items (including sanitary pads) and assured me the teasing would stop. I believed him.

Sometime later, after he confirmed that I did not have a boyfriend, he did the unthinkable. He stole my virginity and then threatened me so I would not tell anyone what he did to me. He told me that if I said anything, we would all be homeless and my mother would hate me. I was fearful for my family, so I remained silent. My stepfather continued the sexual assaults, and I no longer felt safe at home.

I desperately yearned to find my biological father and decided to go on a search for him. Imagine how happy I was when I found him. That motivated me to leave home, as I thought I had found my safety. Unfortunately, that was not the case. After staying with my biological father for a while, he did to me the same thing my stepfather had done. There did not seem to be a safer place for me at the time, so I moved back home with my mother and endured the continued dysfunction.

Reflecting on my challenging upbringing, I remember hearing some older people suggest that "your kids will love you no matter what." The words from that conversation planted a desire and hope deep within my heart that if I had a child, I could receive the type of unconditional love I had been longing for all my life.

When I was in high school, I met a young man at school and decided that I would allow him to be the father of that child. When my mom found out that I was pregnant, she was outraged. She arranged for me to have a private abortion, but I refused to abort the life of the child that would bring me so much love. Even though I knew the baby's father had no love for me or our unborn child, being pregnant allowed me to escape the sexual abuse of my stepfather.

On the other hand, I could not avoid my mother's wrath. Not a day went by when she did not let me know how unhappy she was about my pregnancy. The constant badgering, belittling, and tongue lashings combined with physical abuse were beating me down emotionally and psychologically. On the physical side, I often went to school with scratches on my face and headaches (which lasted for days) due to her pulling my hair. I did not report the abuse for fear that it would make matters worse.

As a young teenage mom, I felt I was falling short. I promised my son that I would give him my best, but I was tired of life, and ending it seemed to be the solution. If I were gone, I thought it would free my son of the shame he faced as a result of having a mother like me. So many times, I talked to a God I hardly believed existed. *If God cared about me, why would he allow me to grow up in such a dysfunctional household? Why did I have to be born into this family?* Those were frequent thoughts throughout my childhood. *There are so many other families I could have been born into—why this one?*

Suicidal thoughts became stronger, and I began to believe that everyone would go on to live happier lives without me. One day, those thoughts overwhelmed me. I went into the bathroom with a razor blade in hand, and I was about to cut my wrist, when my mother walked by. "If you kill yourself, you are going to hell" was all she said.

I felt hopeless, with nowhere to run or hide. I wanted to reach out to the God I had been talking to for all those years, but there were so many times when I didn't even believe he existed. If he existed, why was my life the way it was? In the midst of my despair, something deep inside of me burst forth with a hope that there had to be something better for my life. In that moment, I decided that I had to get away from my dysfunctional home, and even though I didn't know how, I was going to find a way.

My mom did not give me permission to go too many places. Her typical response was, "No! All you're going to do is lay up with some boy and get another baby."

To my surprise, one day she gave me permission to go roller skating with a few of my classmates. I was so excited that I would finally have an opportunity to hang out with my school friends! I had a list of chores to take care of before I would be allowed to go, so I made sure I completed every task on that list and then I checked it twice! I was almost fully dressed and ready to go meet my friends when my mother walked by and asked, "Where do you think you're going?" I could not believe my ears. I was shocked, extremely disappointed, and confused.

At first, I thought maybe I had forgotten to do something that was on the list, or maybe I didn't do it well enough. Whatever the case was, I was willing to do whatever it took to get her to change her mind. I asked her repeatedly, "Why can't I go?" "Because I said so!" was her response each time. I begged her relentlessly to reconsider, and when a surge of boldness flowed through me, I felt I was taking my life in my own hands when I stood in her bedroom door and demanded an answer. I planted myself, blocking her doorway, and even though she walked by me, pushed me, and hit me, I kept my stance. "I know what will move you," she finally said, walking to the closet and pulling out my stepfather's shotgun. I quietly said to myself, "God, I don't know you, but I'm on my way."

My stepfather jumped up from where he was sitting and stopped my mother from shooting me. That night I was told to get out; and I did! I felt abandoned by God. My plan was to never return to that house of pain and abuse again, and even though I didn't know how I was going to make it, I was willing to give it my best try.

During the time when I was going from house to house as a homeless teenage mom, just to have a roof over our heads, I had a lot of time to reflect on my life's many episodes of trauma. The trauma which began with the incident involving my mom shooting my brother, then escalated when my stepfather took my virginity at eleven, continued into my adolescent years. I experienced black eyes, a bloody nose, and I was even thrown from a car in the worst part of town with no way to get home. As reluctant as I was, I accepted a ride from a perfect stranger who reassured me that he would take me to safety. I faced the trauma of fighting off an attacker who took me to the side of a house and attempted to rape me. When the residents of the home heard me screaming for help, they called the police. Trauma seemed to follow me around, but getting kicked out of my mother's house increased my survival skills.

At some point later I began frequently hanging out with a man I met, and although I was sort of in and out but not completely moved away from my mom's house, I was not home very often. This man and I were together for a few years and when he moved away, I moved with him. He ended up cheating on me, so I reluctantly returned to live at my mom's house. Almost immediately after moving back home, I started working at a grocery store. While there, I met another young man. We went on a first date, and on our first encounter, I conceived my second child.

I was so afraid of my mother that the moment I found out I was pregnant again, I knew I could no longer stay at her house. I had to move as soon as possible. The father of my second child and I found a place together, got married, and began attending a church that taught about having a relationship with Christ. I was finally safe! So, I thought.

My second son was born with Holt-Oram syndrome which is a rare genetic disorder that affects the upper limbs and heart. He was born with a hole in his heart and was immediately placed on heart medication. For the first four months of his life, he had to visit a cardiologist every other week. I had not been attending church for very long at that point, but I knew enough to say, "in all things give him thanks." I was thankful for the time I had to spend with my son, but when he died at four months old, I was an emotional wreck.

That was my first experience of losing someone that close to me. After the loss of my son, I could not sleep and was experiencing a tremendous amount of mental and emotional anguish. Have you ever felt like you were doing everything right, but life was still going all wrong? My marriage, with my second son's father, ended shortly after my son's death. At the time of his death, I was six weeks pregnant with my third child. Yes—I was burying one and carrying one at the same time. There was no one around me who could understand the depth of my pain and grief. I was traumatized by life at such a young age and the memories of the trauma still haunted me. Not only was I dealing with the memories of life-long abuse at home, but I was also reflecting on how my search for love and acceptance had led me to even more traumatic experiences. I ended up moving back into my mom's house.

I'm not sure how I did it, but I finally graduated from high school. My next goal was to get out of my mom's house and NEVER look back. It did not happen right away, but I continued to have hope for brighter days.

Still reeling from life's unfair challenges, the failed relationships, and the death of my son, I was feeling very low, and I did what I knew to do. I called on God to help me with the deep pain in my heart caused by my son's absence. It felt like an empty void that NOTHING could fill. But GOD!!

One night, I had a dream, and in the dream, there was a picture that I had of my four-month-old son. The picture came to life right before my eyes and even though he was four months old, he spoke to me! He told me that he loved me, and that his dad and my brother were also there. I asked him to come to me, but he said he couldn't. When I woke up from that dream, I was healed from the pain, the fear, and the uncertainty I had surrounding the heaviness of my son's death. There is still a void in my life in the space where he once occupied, and to this day, I still miss him.

Throughout all of my life's challenges, I give God the honor for keeping me mentally and emotionally sound. I am thankful to have evolved from all of the trauma I experienced with a heart that remains soft, knowing the depths of God's love for me.

God gave me the grace I needed to care for my son as a teenage mom, and the strength I needed to care for my grandma until she passed away. Through God's eyes of love, he also gave me the grace and ability to take care of my mom until she passed. I am thankful for those moments because before she passed, I knew she loved me, and she knew I loved her. God has allowed me to see a message of love in what I once viewed a mess.

No matter what challenge you are facing, there is a message in the end. When I look back on the many challenges I faced, I can see how God's hand was guiding me all the way and how he blessed me with **a second wind**. I am so grateful he has brought me to a place in my life where I am heard, loved, appreciated, and where I know that I matter. Finally!

SECTION II

FROM SHADOWS TO LOVE'S LIGHT

"For you were once darkness, but now you are light in the Lord.
Live as children of light" Ephesians 5:8 NIV

STRIPPED TO THE SOUL

Experiencing God's Rebuilding

LESLIE J COTTRELL

I oversaw care for my parents in their respective declines for over two decades. In February 2023, I faced the emotional task of admitting my mother to hospice services. That weekend, my husband asked me to take a walk with him. Instead of empathy or support, he quickly announced his intention to divorce. My face burned with the frigid winter wind and the scorch of shock. Despite the roaring in my ears, I said, "No!" I tried to swallow, but my throat had gone dry. Again, I said, "No! I have to care for my mother. I need a clear head. So many decisions lie ahead. You can't ask this, NOW!"

My heart knew we had a weak marriage. We were lukewarm together, and I own my part in that. However, he never expressed his desire to rebuild our relationship, or his unhappiness, nor showed any signs that he had thoughts of divorce. He was enjoying his life on his own terms, and I had always accepted that. His intention behind demanding a divorce at that moment could only be to inflict maximum pain. More than a few times over the next few days, I thought my heart would explode in my chest. I was terrified by my bouts of a racing heart, dizziness, and shallow breathing. I tried to look and act normal, but my inner world was crashing within and around me.

We lived in a multi-generational home with my daughter, son-in-law, and granddaughter. They had moved across the country to live with us! Now I faced the rug being ripped out from under them and me. I still feel guilty for exposing them to what I called a carpet bombing. The following few months were excruciating. I concealed news about home from almost everyone, including my mom. I couldn't take a chance of someone telling my mother against my wishes. My drama shouldn't be something she had to navigate at that point in her life. Her dementia made not talking about my situation easier. The hardest part was not answering her frequent questions about my farm animals. Instead, I put all my energy into giving her positive experiences and masked my feelings. Being by her side as she took her last breaths was a heartbreaking blessing. Her last words (about 12 hours before she passed) were a whispered, "Happy Birthday." My birthday was two days away, but she knew she'd be in heaven by then.

The journey of processing multiple losses began. I had to deal with the emotional toll of my mother's death, divorce, farm loss, and uprooting my daughter's family. I could have become bitter and shut down, but God had other plans for me. In Philippians 1:6, we are told that God is faithful to complete the works he started. I believe he started a work within me as a young woman. However, I had turned my direction down a headstrong path years before.

Thankfully, he never abandoned me and was waiting patiently for my return.

I had to take care of my mother's things while navigating what my next career might look like. I had to prioritize redesigning my life over being a "Noni" to my grandchildren as I had intended. Finding new homes for my farm flocks was the saddest part. As much as I longed to ignore reality, I couldn't procrastinate. The last thing I wanted was a hasty decision about their destination. One flock settled on a farm with a young family, the other on a couple's land. Those two departure days were heartbreaking. The sweet animals that I had raised from hatch out were now gone. No more dreams of a farmstead. No more "forever home."

Sitting by our pond, longing to hear my flocks chattering again, I prayed. "God, you are stripping me, stripping me down to my essence. But even through these heartbreaks, I trust you. This all must be for your good. I've been living life on my terms for too long. You've let me try it my way. I want to come home to you. Shape me as you please with what remains. Let me remember this moment whenever I try to take control again. I see you're not finished with me. I understand giving up will not serve you. This can't be the end. I choose you, and I choose your path." The change in my life was palpable.

I hadn't held a job outside the home in some time. Both an illness and time needed with my mother played a part in that. Now I was retirement age. It would have made sense to be living in fight-or-flight mode. Why wasn't I losing it? I had to start from scratch at 66! Even through my prayers, part of me kept waiting for my breakdown. To my amazement, after turning all my worries over to God, the breakdown never came. What was taking place transfixed me. Despite many triggers, I'd feel peaceful, not fearful or angry. My prayer life was deep, unlike in previous years. If I had focused on everything going wrong, I would have been useless to everyone. Shifting my focus to prayer, praise, and gratitude allowed me to navigate the storm without fear of drowning.

My husband refused to move out and stayed until the divorce was final and the house sold. That decision introduced another oppressive layer of stress and angst for everyone in our house. I hated exposing my kids to the constant pressure. Honestly, I was unsure how to proceed, but God gave me another lifeline. One morning, while in prayer, I felt His presence saying, "Give yourself silence. You do not have to engage. You can be silent." Much to my husband's frustration, that is what I did. We lived with him in silence. He took it as a personal affront, but that was not my concern. I needed to avoid arguments and potentially more upheaval in the house. His selfishness made me feel sick, and our conversations would become heated. Those few moments of heat encouraged me to continue to stay in silence and keep my thoughts to myself. Every time losses overwhelmed me I turned to God in prayer. He became my confidant and my strength. It was not my first divorce, but now I owned my worth and stood my ground. I refused to turn over and make things easy for my husband's comfort. I let my attorney handle communication and I focused on rebuilding my life.

In 2019, my good friend was preparing to launch a publishing business. She and I met in 2016 and became fast friends. We worked as freelancers for the same publishing business and admired one another's value systems. We discussed a publishing venture, but I had to prioritize being accessible to my mother. It was the right choice then. I needed to be available to care for Mom during emergencies, and there were many. If I had joined the business then, I couldn't have achieved all I wanted and would disappoint my friend. Or, I wouldn't have been able to be present for my mother's needs as she deserved and needed.

Now I felt the Lord leading me to call her, so I sat in that same spot by the pond and dialed her number. I told her I was ready to get involved in the business if she needed me. What happened next was of God, not of me. I announced that my intention was not just to work for the company, but also to invest. Of course, at that time I didn't know how much money I would have to invest! What was I thinking? As the words left my mouth, I felt an overwhelming sense of peace. Over the next few months, we talked together, and, despite my life's uncertainty, God led me to escalate the amount I was committing to invest. Making business plans was wonderful medicine and brought glimmerings of hope for my new life. I committed to a financial obligation without even knowing my future. I was living in faith, and it was one of the most liberating experiences of my life.

I am so blessed that my children decided they still wanted to live together with me as a family. The pain caused by the end of my marriage made me doubt if they still wanted to do that, but I believe God softened their hearts. It had always been our dream to provide a village to raise their children.

I worked hard to get the house ready for the market. The property was beautiful but catered to a specific personality. It was my goal to make the viewing experience faultless so its quirky beauty could shine through. Having no new place to live, listing the house demanded even greater faith. Suddenly, the house was under contract within the first five days. The clock was ticking down! We established a "drop dead" date for being under contract for a new house and the Sunday of that last weekend, we found it! It was our blessing house. Again, the Lord provided. Time after time, God was the sole answer to our provisions. I declared I'd never doubt God's care for me again. This story was written one year after the divorce was final.

My testimony is not one with fireworks. Don't we just love those dramatic salvation and re-commitment stories? Although my story is more subtle, it is nothing short of amazing. My story doesn't involve experiences on the streets, with addiction, homelessness, or mental instability. My testimony is rooted in the day I spent by the pond. Every day since then, I have moved forward in faith. My dream life is now a reality. It's not because I won the lottery and have a big house on the ocean or a fancy car. My life's purpose shifted. With that pivotal moment, everything clicked into focus like the second an optometrist snaps your perfect lenses into place. It would have been easy to suppress my testimony because it isn't flashy, but I have realized that in times of challenge, we either live in faith and prayer or fear. There is no middle ground. I could change none of what happened in my life, but I could change how it affected my life. It's not trite when we hear the phrase, *life is what we make of it*. Attitude is the driving force behind how we either grow or wither. Alone, I couldn't possess the ability to embrace grace and gratitude. It came from re-surrendering my life to God.

Today, we live in a sweet little house with a new baby coming. Our home is peaceful, creative, and filled with joy. I am the chief operating officer of a publishing services company and a best-selling book-writing coach. I've fallen in love with helping new writers bring their stories to life.

Know that life's challenges will never stop coming. The enemy will never run out of energy to sabotage your relationship with God. What made that day at the pond significant? For once, I kept nothing for myself. I don't believe I had ever done that before. I always kept something in reserve that was mine alone. The enemy found a foothold in that reserve, leading me away from the Lord. Even that was subtle. I always took pride in how "spiritual" I was. Sadly, I was chasing after the next best thing in man's version of spirituality instead of simply serving God. It took my life crumbling for me to gain clarity on how misguided I was.

Through being stripped to my soul, I have grown deeper in my obedience and faith. Aligning with God's will gives me the ability to discern good from bad, and enriching from depleting. I am not obligated to give energy to anything that does not enrich me. I am more emotionally resilient now and seldom influenced by what is happening around me. Great joy fills my life, which is not determined by material possessions.

My faith has become unshakeable, but it is something I don't take for granted. To have this in your life, you must nurture your spiritual garden through prayer and reading God's word. This discipline will affect all aspects of your life. You'll see your resolve become stronger, which to some may look like self-control. My patience has grown through prayer and letting go. Do you see the common denominator here? Faith is the ribbon that runs through spiritual growth. Jesus owed me absolutely nothing. He already gave me his everything on the cross. Logically, he should have shunned me and not cared about my well-being. However, the moment I surrendered to him, he held me in his arms like the prodigal daughter I was. This knowledge is humbling.

Peace and comfort follow those who have exited my life, for I know their season ended. I can absorb their lessons and then let them go.

> *The Lord said: forget what happened long ago! Don't think about the past. I am creating something new. There it is! Do you see it? I have put roads in deserts, streams in thirsty lands. Isaiah 43: 18-19 (CEV)*

By placing my trust in God with small things, he granted me bigger opportunities to follow him. Through challenges, I grew and experienced more blessings.

> *Anyone who can be trusted in little matters can also be trusted in important matters. But anyone who is dishonest in little matters will be dishonest in important matters. If you cannot be trusted with this wicked wealth, who will trust you with true wealth? And if you cannot be trusted with what belongs to someone else, who will give you something that will be your own? You cannot be the slave of two masters. You will like one*

more than the other or be more loyal to one than to the other.
You cannot serve God and money. Luke 16: 10-14

May you find your own way to turn to God during those storms that threaten to reshape your future. I wonder what would've happened if I hadn't let go of control over my life. I suspect it would have turned out differently. Perhaps I would have stayed in a resentful and angry frame of mind for the rest of my days. It's easy to envision how that stormy season could have shaped the rest of my life, but I am so grateful for **my second wind**. I am thankful that my story is one of peace, joy, and deep fulfillment. I cannot imagine a better legacy for my children, grandchildren, and beyond.

REBIRTH OF THE QUEEN

REGINA NICHELLE

Like a film playing in slow motion, I can still see her—that long-legged, doe-eyed little girl, innocent and hopeful. During her "pretending" games, she always chose the name Elizabeth to be her name. There was magic in that name. Queen Elizabeth's power, grace, and quiet authority enchanted her, illuminating the belonging and acceptance that she didn't feel. She wanted desperately to be valued and seen, but as the child from a previous relationship, she bore a different last name. It was a subtle yet undeniable reminder that she was set apart, the lone piece that didn't quite fit into her own family. It may have been a small difference through the eyes of some, but to her, it was a monumental difference. Not only did the world see her as different, but she felt it in every interaction with "him." She thought the voices were only in her head, but maybe "he" heard those voices too. The voices chanted that she wasn't good enough to be there, and his agreement with them left more hurt than one little girl could process.

Over the years she met those voices with a focused resolve that ultimately left its own wounds. Fueled by a yearning to feel worthy of love and acceptance, she strived for achievement. She was good enough and she would make them see. She would prove them wrong. Despite the scholarships, the titles, the outwardly successful image, nothing silenced them. The thrill of each new accomplishment quickly faded, leaving her emptier. The void born out of lack of relationship ironically couldn't be filled by relationship. She dated the cute, the popular, the smart, and the athletes. Her struggle with trust and self-worth only increased as none of them could remain faithfully committed to her. Instead, each relationship ended with another heartbreak, another rejection, and another assault to her self-worth. Did they all hear the voices, too? On the outside, she was a goal oriented, high achiever; but inside, a wounded little girl was at the helm deciding all the moves.

With anticipation and great expectation, I embraced a new start. My marriage set the stage for the American dream wrapped in a handsome husband, a beautiful suburban home, two vehicles, an adorable healthy baby boy, even a dog. I had anticipated that this relationship would be different. In a lot of ways, he was different than the others, but he wasn't different enough for me. I don't know exactly when the happy days became long, lonely nights; but those nights eventually became mornings overwhelmed by work, caring for kids, fretting over finances, and arguing.

Far too many mornings, I had to put on my big girl panties while holding it all together by a thread. There were mornings that couldn't sneak up on me because I was waiting for them with eyes wide open, too stressed to sleep. There were other mornings that calls from creditors awakened me instead of the alarm clock. I still remember the morning I was awakened by a strange noise outside. As I went to investigate, I peered through the blinds just in time to see my car being towed away. Just like me, my bank account was empty. I didn't even have time or energy to cry about it. On that morning, like so many others, I covered the pain with some Mary Kay and kept moving.

That became my routine, until infidelity became an issue. In the past, it was rejection that fueled my determination to succeed, each pushing me harder to prove them wrong. As the rejection piled up, the defiance gradually was replaced by disappointment. The harder I fought, the louder the voices screamed "You're just not enough!" I was running out of fight. The bitter taste of resignation began to settle in. Maybe the voices were right. The possibility that I really wasn't enough made me angry. I became angry at everyone who had rejected me. I became angry at myself for allowing it. The more I internalized the resentment, the more it poisoned my emotions. The hurt, anger and despair weighed me down emotionally and physically, my body carried my brokenness and damaged self-worth as pounds. Ironically, unlike the men in my life, the pounds were committed to me. They wouldn't go anywhere. They should have been able to insulate me from additional hurt, but the rejection came from inside. That had become my life.

Numbly pushing forward, I was pregnant with my second child. I remember the night he was conceived. I can't explain what I felt or how I knew, but I was sure something was different. In my ignorance, I didn't realize just how my life would change, and it didn't take long.

An extreme pain in my calf forced me to go see my doctor. I almost left the doctor's office out of frustration because the wait was so long, and as soon I got up to leave, a very audible voice told me to sit down. After some time, I was taken to an exam room and minutes after the doctor walked into the room, I passed out. I moved back and forth between consciousness while I was being transported to the hospital. I later discovered a blood clot had travelled to my heart. What if I'd not listened to that voice?

Exhausted and broken, no longer able to hold it all in, I cried out to God. I cried because I desperately needed help with the mess of a life I had created. I had tried to do everything right, but things were far from right. As I angrily yelled at God, I heard the same voice that spoke to me from the doctor's office calmly but clearly say, "I never told you to marry him." Touche! It was a hard truth, but it made things crystal clear. Ironically, that life and the twelve-year marriage ended over Easter weekend, the ultimate picture of death and resurrection. Twelve is the number of completion. Beginnings always require an ending. The end was the beginning, and the beginning of many endings.

Like the start of labor pains, a change was stirring. That was the day my water broke. It was a symbolic turning point for me and the beginning of my transformation. Birthing is hard and messy work. The often long, painful and sometimes tearful process requires great strength as newness comes to life. My contractions had begun and the pain was unbearable!

Julian's life, began with Down's syndrome and multiple holes in his heart, which closely mirrored the brokenness of my own. My mornings were full of financial strains, heartache, frustration, disappointment, rejection, and fighting. I was exhausted, frustrated, and numb, especially with the additional challenges of doctor visits, therapy sessions, emergency room visits, and surgeries. It all became more than one little girl could process.

Despite the seizures and numerous holes in Julian's heart requiring surgery when he was only weeks old, he was exceeding all expectations. But, Julian developed pneumonia. I was so exhausted that I don't recall when nights turned to days. When he began improving, I reluctantly returned him to the sitters so that I could try to work. During my class, I got a call from Julian's sitter. "He's asleep now, but something isn't right," she said. I returned home immediately to find Julian still in the crib. When I went picked him up, he was unresponsive. I faintly remember the frantic call to 911 and desperately performing CPR on his limp little body until the medics arrived. A police officer drove me to the hospital as the ambulance sped off. I knew what they never had to tell me. His death was an unimaginable loss.

That afternoon and the weeks that followed are still a blur. I expected, and even welcomed, the end of my marriage; but I never expected to lose my baby to heart failure when it was my heart that was failing. I don't have words to describe the depth of that pain. I was dazed and so very numb and the contractions continued. Less than two months after burying my baby, I found myself unemployed, bankrupt and facing eviction with a young child to care for. Then Sasha, our dog, died. Within six months my life had completely imploded. With bad credit, no job, my son Zachary, and our truck, the journey began.

I relocated to a beautiful, newly renovated townhome. My landlord was God-sent. He worked with me and even finished the basement space to accommodate my sister. He said I reminded him of a family friend who experienced a similar tragedy and showed me so much favor. I began the difficult and long road to healing, which has taken years. When I released the emotional baggage, my body began to release some of the physical weight I had carried for so long. Those contractions were hard but eventually they squeezed out every lie that the enemy tried to make me believe. The Queen was born!

Gina, that wounded little girl who once pretended to be Elizabeth, had lived through the fire and emerged transformed. Her mother had unknowingly prophesied over her life: the name Regina means queen. "Re" means once again. She had been given a divine do-over. She no longer needed to pretend to be a queen; she had become one. Shaped by the trials and refined by God's grace.

Zachary was and continues to be an invaluable part of my rebirth. Within days of Julian's death, I watched a news report of a woman who had lost both of her children in a car accident. Instead of being angry over my loss, I could only thank God that I still had Zachary. For some reason, God had entrusted me with this precious boy who needed me. Despite my brokenness, I couldn't fail either of them. Yes, Zachary needed me; but I needed him so much more. God gave me the name for him, Zachary DeShawn. Zachary which means God has remembered. I didn't quite understand before; but now I get it. God remembered that little girl. God remembered her hurt. God remembered her shame. God remembered her rejection. But more importantly, God remembered that he had placed a queen within her. In His infinite wisdom He gave me Zachary to restore my self-worth and value and make sure I stayed the course on the assignment chosen just for me. DeShawn means God is gracious.

Queen Esther didn't have her daddy around; but that didn't stop her either. She ascended from being an orphaned slave girl to the throne in a foreign land. She was a powerful vessel whose reign was marked by selfless devotion to God and her people. Chosen by God to serve, she humbly and empathetically brought deliverance to her people. Like Esther, I have turned the pain of my life into purpose. I'm moving into spaces that the world says I'm not supposed to be, places that those voices tried to talk me out of. I can walk boldly with confidence now that I have dispelled the lies and silenced the chanting. No more seeking approval and acceptance. No more compromising and discounting my own value. No more striving for achievement in order to feel valued. I know who I am. I know whose I am. It takes balance and an erect back to wear this crown. I move confidently knowing that my Father is with me. How funny is it to now realize that daddy issues caused me so much pain even though Daddy God was always there?

My rebirth brought meaning not just in my own healing but in my purpose to empower others. With newfound strength, in 2020 I established Mpowerd, a nonprofit created to empower single mothers to build strong futures for themselves and their families. We help them recognize their true identity and value so they, too, can rule and reign in life.

Esther's beauty treatments lasted months, but it took years to remove the residue from my old life and prepare me for the throne.

It took a lot of change–change in mindset, change in behaviors, and change in habits to begin to operate in God's purpose for my life. My focus had to change. My confidence had to change. However, nothing was wasted. The experience impassioned me to bring value even in the marketplace as I help people and organizations make and sustain changes that will push them into their destiny.

My heart breaks every time I hear of a mother who has lost a child. The pain is still indescribable. Yet, I can now sing praises despite the loss. Julian also was named by God; Julian means victor. We sometimes forget that there's no victory without a fight. Julian Christopher fought hard every day of his 19 months. Christopher means "bearing Christ" and likewise, his life was not in vain, and His death was not a loss. Just as Christ's victory came by way of the grave and from it we have access to life. I know with certainty that Julian's death pushed me into this new life. Romans 8:28 says "And we know that all things work together for good to them that love God, to them who are the called according to His purpose." Even after losing so much, I've won. The birthing is complete. God gave **me a second wind**. The devil thought he could stop me, but he should have killed me when he had the chance. Now my mornings are filled with praise and thanksgiving. Joy cometh in the morning!

The words of a queen are powerful. Bringing favor or judgment, they carry authority and demand obedience. I declare life, healing and deliverance to you as you read these words. I assure you that joy can be your portion as well. God is no respecter of persons. He has a plan for your life, and purpose even for your pain. To the woman who feels unseen, unheard, and unvalued, know that you are more than enough. To those who have made mistakes, endured heartache, and felt broken, your story is far from over. To the fatherless and unloved, you are not alone. God, our Father, had a plan for you even before you were in your mother's womb, and He will see it through. Just as God was present with me all along the way, He will never leave your side. When my life was literally falling apart, God was putting those pieces together to make something beautiful. He can make a masterpiece of your broken pieces, too.

There is no easy road. Esther's path to the throne was filled with hardship. She didn't ask for that life, but she was built for it. It made her the queen that she proved to be. Everything that she needed was within her.

My second wind journey echoes a message of resilience and purpose, serving as a reminder to women everywhere that you won't be exempt from the pain, but you, too, are more than enough. Dig deep because everything you need is inside of you. Dust yourself off and put on your crown. You are a queen—so walk like one.

RELEASED FROM THE SHACKLES OF A BROKEN COVENANT

ROBIN A. HILL

I ended the call abruptly and angrily threw my phone down. The truth hit me so hard it knocked the wind right out of me. I gathered my breath right before I doubled over and began sobbing uncontrollably. As the night settled into my bedroom, I felt like my hurting heart was being ripped from my chest. My world, as I knew it, was flipped upside down like an episode of *The Twilight Zone*. I was living in a physiological twist of reality in a religious world of smoke and mirrors. You see, my husband and I were pastoring a church, and his affair was exposed by the hard cold facts that tore down the façade that hid the lies, betrayal, and deception.

Many thoughts flooded my mind concerning why he would break our covenant. I would have to agree with Aristotle's argument that everything in the universe must have a cause and with every cause, there is an effect. Although we all have free will to choose our path, our choices are always influenced by someone or something. Being an offspring of adultery, my husband chose to disregard the U-Turn, No Trespassing, and Wrong Way Road signs in life's travels.

Consequently, he kept going until he crashed our marriage right into a dead end leaving behind mangled memories and the dilapidated remains of two marriages. Yes, she was married too!

Frequently being a damsel in distress. My hero of a husband (the Pastor) was always at her beck and call. They found more and more projects that involved only the two of them. I saw the smoke, but his ministerial cloak blinded my view of the fire. Her husband expressed his belief (several times) that a man and woman who were not married to each other should not be alone together. Consequently, her husband became increasingly attached to her. I was surprised that she called me one day seeking my advice. During our conversation, she told me that her husband's clinging had become unbearable. She was planning to "put him away" for psychiatric evaluation. That night, her husband unfortunately died of an overdose caused by a drug that only she administered. Her desire to "put him away" took a fatal turn.

After her husband's death, several inappropriate actions and interactions between her and my husband transpired. He brazenly added her to our family cell phone plan. Their unrestrained outings together increased, no longer limited by her late husband. She was given a position to minister alongside him on Sundays, despite her lack of ministerial training or experience, while I (with years of experience as a licensed and ordained minister), was sidelined without any explanation.

One particular Friday, I was experiencing flu symptoms. I called my husband to ask him to pick me up early from work. After several unsuccessful attempts to reach him, a coworker drove me home.

Feeling achy and feverish, I needed him, so I followed my intuition when I got out of my co-worker's car and walked straight to her apartment. When I arrived, I found her front door oddly ajar, I stepped inside, said, "Hello?" and called out her name. Hearing no response, I walked back to her bedroom door. I called her name again and was met with silence. With a sinking feeling, I slowly opened the door. There she was, lying on the bed. My eyes slowly traveled from her feet to her head in that dimly lit room. There he was at the head of her bed rubbing his fingers through her hair and eerily praying in tongues. The sacredness of prayer intertwined with that perverse scene caused me to feel even sicker.

In that southern town, I blotted out the gossip about a Black pastor and a White laywoman sighted at a neighboring hotel, because it was hearsay! I used my husband's claims of innocence to silence my intuitional alarms, and concerning his imbecilic actions I quoted "Love covers a multitude of faults" in my mind. To no avail, I communicated how his actions did not align with our ministerial training. I also asked him, "What if I behaved with a man the way you behave with her?" Using his position of authority, his response was, "Being the senior minister, you can't do what I do."

Our final argument was about her throwing him a birthday party; inappropriately buying him cologne; and not inviting me, his wife, to the party. What infuriated me even more was that he saw nothing wrong with it. The argument almost turned violent as every snide, cold, arrogant remark he made tempted me to jab him right in the throat. When he said, "Why don't you just leave?" Immediately I heard God's whisper, *"That's enough."* From that moment, I stopped talking, and I moved out the following week.

Thinking my move would be temporary, I left pretty much everything behind.

While we were separated, my prayer was that the Lord would convict him concerning salvaging our marriage and ministry. I waited in limbo for a call from him to discuss our past, present, or future, but that phone call never happened. He did manage to call about adding more non-family members to our cell phone plan, which prompted me to go to the phone company to have my name removed from that polygamous family plan. Unbeknownst to me, I was the account holder and was able to access the phone records, uncovering an even deeper layer of my husband's hidden secrets.

The phone records revealed that for months, while I slept in our marriage bed, my husband and his mistress secretly talked in the wee hours of the morning. They talked during his drive to and from his job and throughout the night when he worked the third shift. Finally, the veil was removed from my eyes. **HE HAD RE-PLACED ME--IN MY FACE!** The dagger that penetrated even deeper was the discovery that they spoke twenty-two times on my birthday, but on that day, I remember being sad because he didn't call me once.

Feeling perturbed, I called him to tell him about my findings. I reminded him of our covenant before God and demanded an apology. He haughtily refused, as if twenty-six years of marriage meant nothing to him. Running through my mind like a ticker tape was everything I had done for him, the ministry, and all I had suffered. I was enraged when I promised to expose the affair before the congregation. And if he didn't give me an open apology, I was prepared to flip chairs, yell and fight. I even encouraged him to call the cops because he might need them. Motivated by wrath and half an IQ, I wanted revenge. While spewing my angry intent, I felt like *The Incredible Hulk*, but after the call, I doubled over and sobbed like a baby.

Through my tears, I saw a bright glowing presence drift into my dark bedroom and then dissipate like a mist. Immediately God spoke to me and said, *"You are only doing this to feel better about what was done. You will **never** feel good about what was done."* Instantly I understood that any act of vengeance on my part would be useless because the paradigm would never change. God then said, *"Leave it alone and let me heal you".* And concluded by saying, *"Vengeance is mine!"* Broken, I obeyed his command and let the matter go. I then sensed the warm hand of the Comforter soothing my hurting heart. I stopped crying and fell into a deep sleep. When I woke up the next morning, I was fully rested, something I had not experienced in almost two years.

A short time after, I discovered there were other mistresses—some were much younger. Reflecting on the shocking revelations of my husband's secret double life caused me to literally lose a day. I felt mentally trapped in a realm of torment, where every lash of betrayal, humiliation, neglect, abandonment, rejection, and disrespect cut deeply, each tied to those who had shared our marriage bed. The lies and deception debased every cherished memory and milestone of our marriage, reducing the value of being his wife to that of discarded trash. When I finally regained mental clarity, I knew I desperately needed help to overcome the heart-wrenching challenge before me—and I needed much more than just a pep talk!

I was emotionally raw, and as I desperately sought God for his divine intelligence to guide me, His instruction to forgive and show mercy was the most crucial aspect of my recovery. The act of forgiveness removed my feelings of entitlement to any covenant, vow, or debt owed to me. I understood that mercy was not deserved, but the act of extending mercy helped me to become emotionally detached from the offense and offender—as if they never existed.

To maintain a heart of peace, devoid of the clutter of bad feelings, meditation, and prayer became my daily practice. When a memory triggers bad feelings, I mentally release mercy, like releasing a white sheet to cover the offense and offender from my mind's eye. This practice produces a barrier against emotions like anger and resentment. On purpose, I focus only on the truth. Embracing truth and showing mercy remains my ticket to receiving favor and good understanding from God and mankind Proverbs 3:3-4 KJV).

After reflecting on Psalm 118:8, I felt inspired to make another significant shift in my lifestyle—place my trust solely in God. In prayer, the Lord made it comprehensively clear that He should be the only one on the throne of my heart. As Lord of my life, He decides what is allowed to come into my heart and what needs to leave, ensuring that no lies or negative emotions take root. I have permitted God to remove anything in my heart that is not aligned with Him, and I measure my interactions with others by the fruit of the Spirit described in Galatians 5:22-23. I choose to live without allowing offenses to negatively impact me. *"Great peace have they which love thy law: and nothing shall offend them."* Psalm 119:165 (KJV)

I am now enlightened that my husband taking pleasure in others does not define my self-worth. My self-worth is firmly rooted in my identity as a daughter of God. God abiding in me makes me a walking miracle. As His daughter, I live with the exuberance of His Spiritual DNA. It empowers me to rise above negativity and embrace a space where joy, faith, great expectation, and divine intelligence thrive. The truth from God's word has separated me from negativity. *"Sanctify them through thy truth: thy word is truth."* John 17:17.

God's truth has empowered me to love and appreciate myself. I spend my time with people who celebrate my gifts, talents, and the beauty of who I am as created by God, rather than with those who merely tolerate my presence. My preferences take precedence over what I once acquiescently accepted, and I live in a space of creative freedom where inspiring and uplifting others ignites my passion for writing. I have authored several books and written and recorded a song titled *That's Why I Praise You.* I embrace every opportunity that God provides for me to serve as a keynote speaker, I host women empowerment events, founded the Lady Lexus Club (a luxury car networking organization), and established a virtual book club entitled 52 Weeks of Purposeful Thinking.

Released from the shackles of a broken covenant, I was ready to live like who I was meant to be. However, before entering another relationship, I had two questions I needed clarity regarding my status as a divorcee. My first question was, "Lord, you told us to marry. Will being divorced take me outside of your perfect will?" In my search through God's word for the answer, I jumped up and down on my bed when I read Deuteronomy 24:2, which clearly explains that if divorced, a woman is free to be another man's wife. My second question to God was, "Why did you tell me to marry him, knowing we'd divorce?" His answer was simple, *"If you didn't go through everything you went through, I would not be able to use you the way I am using you now."* To further confirm the answer to my questions, I was at church one Sunday, when a pastor gave me a word from God. He said, *"Your husband altered my instructions, like Adam. In the same way, Christ is Adam's substitute, I am going to send you a substitute, and, like Christ, the substitute is better!"*

The answers and confirmation I received brought complete peace to my heart. After five years of living as a divorcee, I felt whole and ready to marry again. Before meeting that special someone, the Lord guided me to make another significant lifestyle change; one that I whole-heartedly obeyed. *"Only think and say what you want to manifest in your future,"* was God's instruction. I understood that every thought and word I expressed needed to align with what I truly wanted to bring into my life! If I wanted God's best, it was my responsibility to guard against being double-minded and stay focused. I passionately meditated on scriptures like Proverbs 12:14, Proverbs 18:21, and Psalm 37:4, which helped anchor my thoughts.

In my heart, I knew the type of man I was expecting to enter my life, and I was preparing myself to receive him. I was looking for a man whose heart belonged to God and was controlled by God. He would possess the divine intelligence to know how to love, cherish, and adore me, and he would be the perfect fit for the woman I have been cultivated to be. A few months after adjusting to align my thoughts and words, I met a wonderful man who was more than I imagined and declared! In 2015 we got married and have since then grown together in every aspect of our lives. We are building three businesses together that offer health and wellness products and services, including consultations, workshops, and events for couples and singles. We offer books, plant-based skincare, and healthy delicious spice blends as well. Our marriage, guided by faith in God's divine presence, tells a beautiful story, radiating love, joy, and unity, wherever we go.

God's divine intelligence has released me from the shackles of a broken covenant. I navigate life's challenges with precision and have established new habits that promote wellness. With God on the throne of my heart, I reject lies and negative emotions. I gauge my actions and interactions with others by the fruit of the Spirit and focus my thoughts and words on what I wish to manifest. I embrace a life of health, wealth, true love, and the bliss of heaven right here on earth. I am very grateful - I got my **2nd Wind!**

BETRAYED BY LOVE

SARA OMAYA AGAK

I returned home after studying abroad for about four and a half years. After breaking off my engagement with my fiancé (a story for another time, but needs to be told!), I had no interest whatsoever in settling down with anyone or pursuing any kind of relationship with a man—period! I was settling into my new role as a hospital pharmacist, leaving me with little time for other activities.

One day, a gentleman confidently walked up to the pharmacy window and asked to speak to the pharmacist in charge. I was the pharmacist in charge. He had no appointment, was carrying no laptop or notebook, or anything that might indicate he wanted to discuss business. He was very well groomed, with a playful smile and an air of self-confidence that was intoxicating. I politely informed him that meetings were strictly by appointment only and he immediately booked the next available slot to see me. *Would you not want to listen to such a confident, self-assured man?* I asked myself. And so began my relationship with Alex, the man with a disarming smile.

The amount of time and effort he put into pursuing me was very flattering. After months of daily calls, texts, and impromptu visits to the hospital under the guise that he was meeting other healthcare providers within the hospital, he eventually asked me out on a date. I accepted his invitation—I was intrigued!

During our first meaningful conversation, he revealed that he had a child from a previous relationship and that he was estranged from his child based on the wishes of his ex-girlfriend. I was impressed that he was willing to be so honest and vulnerable early on in our relationship. He put himself out there, knowing there was a possibility that I might reject him because of his situation. *If he can be so honest and open this soon in the relationship, he must definitely be into me,* I thought.

After that conversation, I felt special, loved, and comfortable enough to move forward in our relationship. I was all in and fell in love with him much sooner than I had anticipated!

A few months later, I remember being curled up in my favorite chair in the living room of my one-bedroom apartment on a cold and rainy Saturday morning. With a cup of steaming hot chocolate, I was lost in thought about how much I loved Alex and how much I missed him when he was not around. I was consumed with my love reflections for so long that my hot chocolate had gone cold, prompting me to head to the kitchen for a refill. While my thoughts were mostly filled with love, a nagging question lingered in the back of my mind: *Was Alex truly my Mr. Right?* As I refreshed my hot chocolate, my loving thoughts shifted to rumors I'd heard about the man I was preparing to marry.

My thoughts switched from feeling deeply in love to questioning whether I should pay attention to the rumors. *Was there any truth to them? Should I continue with our wedding plans, or wait until I felt more confident about my decision to marry Alex?* Although I had met a few members of his family, I hadn't yet been introduced to his mother or sister. *Should that concern me?* I couldn't stop wondering.

Deep down, I felt meeting them would signify a stable relationship, their blessing, and a clear path to move forward with the wedding. Not long after that introspective morning, I received devastating news that turned my world upside down.

One evening, Alex stopped by my apartment on his way home from work to use my computer. He wanted to catch up on some personal e-mails which was nothing out of the ordinary because we practically spent every minute of every hour together. I prepared dinner while he used my computer, and when he was done, we had dinner together. As usual, we had a pleasant conversation and when it was time for him to leave, he kissed me goodbye and off he went. I went about my evening routine and about two hours later, I was fast asleep.

I wasn't very active on social media, so a few days later, I decided to spend some time to catch up on my personal emails. When I sat down to log in to my computer, I noticed that Alex never logged out. What I did next is not something I'm proud of, but curiosity got the better of me. I betrayed Alex's trust and skimmed through the email headings. When my eyes landed upon one subject line, in particular, I froze dead in my tracks. ***Our wedding photos.***

I initially thought one of his friends had shared wedding photos with him, so I clicked on the link. There, I saw Alex (the groom) alongside a beautiful woman dressed as the bride. I was stunned. The groom (Alex) was surrounded by his best man, brothers, sister and mother, while the bride stood with her bridal party and family. Tears streamed down my face, but I was too shocked to make a sound. I was frozen in disbelief, my body trembling as I collapsed to my knees. Then a chorus of agonized cries filled my ears--cries of betrayal, cries of anguish pleading, *"How could he do this to me?"*

A hollow ache settled in the pit of my stomach, as though life was being drained from me in agonizing waves. I felt like a mere shell of myself. How could the man I had invested in emotionally and physically, and was prepared to commit to for a lifetime, turn out to be married? Was it some kind of cruel joke? Lying on the floor, I wept uncontrollably, feeling my heart fracture, one teardrop at a time.

What was even more difficult was that when I discovered this betrayal, Alex had been admitted to the hospital because he was ill. When I confronted him about the wedding photos, he denied, denied, and denied that he was married. He was so convincing in his full-blown gaslighting mode that I began doubting the wedding photos and video that I had seen with my own eyes. Our phone conversations from his hospital bed over the next few days were laced with anger, hurt, bitterness, disappointment, and sadness. I remember that sunny Saturday morning when the brightness outside stood in stark contrast to the storm that was raging within me. I felt consumed by darkness, pain, anger, vulnerability, and a deep disappointment in myself.

Suddenly, the doorbell rang, catching me off guard since I was not expecting anyone. When I opened the front door, I was completely dumbstruck to see Alex standing there, out of breath and visibly frail. He had discharged himself from the hospital, against medical advice, determined to "save our relationship." My anger surged as I watched him struggle to stay upright, but mindful of the prying eyes of the neighbors, I managed to suppress my emotions just enough to let him inside. I just didn't like airing my dirty laundry to the world.

When he stepped inside, he was sweating like a horse and looked like he would lose consciousness at any minute. I invited him to sit, and I sat across from him. I just watched him, without saying a word. I did not trust myself to speak in a civil manner, so I waited for him to break the silence. Eventually, he spoke, in the form of an apology. He apologized for deceiving me and for denying that he was married. A part of me was still in denial that I had fallen victim to that level of deception. I had been so careful and thought I had found an honest man, but as painful as it was, I said goodbye to him and braced myself to begin another chapter of my life without him. He had said everything he came to say, and I was firm in my refusal to take him back.

At first, life without him was empty. I was so used to getting a text from him in the morning and throughout the day and on most evenings, we would see each other after work. Our weekends were filled with trips out of town, spending time together watching movies, cooking together, and lots of laughter. It all came to an abrupt end, and there were many nights I cried myself to sleep.

Other nights I would just lay awake in bed and relive the painful moments, asking myself, *"How did you miss it?"*

I set out on the road to recovery, determined to not repeat the same mistake, ever again.

I immersed myself in fictional novels, spent more time visiting my parents, changed jobs, and began pursuing a master's in health systems management. The job changes and my studies kept me incredibly busy, as my weekdays were filled with work and night classes, while Saturdays often consisted of all-day lectures. My routine became a continuous cycle of coming home, tackling homework and group projects, heading to bed (sometimes too exhausted to eat), waking up, and doing it all over again. I made new friends, and whenever time permitted, we would go out for lunch together. Growing closer to God included me dedicating time to daily devotions and attending church every Sunday. I participated in a 10-week program designed to explore our Christian roots. During that time, a worship group was formed, and we met weekly to share life updates and strengthen our connection to God's work. Gradually, I began to heal.

A few months after the break-up, Alex reached out to me. He wanted to know who the best oncologist in the country was, and he used that opportunity to let me know he had been diagnosed with cancer. I put aside my anger, my pain, my hurt and my disappointment and chose to walk with him on his journey, step-by-step as he started treatment. On the days of his chemo treatments, I dashed home from work in the evenings, grabbed a quick shower and dinner, then rushed to the hospital before visiting hours ended. While I was there with him, we talked (on the days when he was not too weak to talk). For so many days I sat next to him, watching him sleep or writhe in pain, and the only thing I could do was hold his hand and pray for him to go into remission.

One day while I was there, he received a visit from one of his colleagues. During the round of introductions, she very innocently asked "Oh, is this your wife?" I was unable to attend your wedding, so it is such a pleasure to finally meet you face-to-face."

You could have heard a pin drop! Alex had denied on so many occasions that he was married, and in walks a colleague who unknowingly unraveled a lie. God heard my silent cries and answered me loud and clear by sending me the next best thing–a colleague, to demystify things between Alex and me and eliminate any doubt I may have had about who he was. Alex did all the talking while I stayed quiet. I put on a forced poker face as I listened to their conversation, holding back my anger, pain, and tears. I recalled the morning I was so caught up in my thoughts about Alex that my mug of hot chocolate got cold, and one of the questions I had been pondering was being answered. As their small talk continued, I took it all in stride but silently thanked God. *You have come through, and I have heard you loudly and clearly.*

After that visit, Alex stopped denying that he was married, and as painful as it was, I honored my commitment to see him through to the end of his treatment. Three years later, he went into remission and went to join his wife abroad. After he left, I held a board meeting with myself to consciously chart out the next phase of my life and how I planned to get there.

I resolved to work on two very important relationships: my relationship with God, and my relationship with myself. I vowed to get to know and understand what it means to have a close relationship with God and to learn to trust Him in every area of my life. I was also determined to do more than just chart a way forward for myself, but to develop a vision board for my life (including my dream job) and affirm myself as each goal materialized. I was on the road to recovery and one day, out of the blue, I heard from Alex. He was home on vacation and reached out to me.

In a short conversation, I told him it was not the best of times for me because I had just buried my dad a few days prior. He accused me of lying to him! For a moment, I felt the sting of that all-too-familiar pain that only he could inflict. As I tried to make sense of his response, he deleted the message and sent a more appropriate one. In that moment, even though I was still filled with the grief of losing my father, I saw very clearly that God had protected me from continuing in a relationship that would have been filled with doubt and me questioning my sense of reality at every turn.

Not all decisions are the right ones, but I honored my vow to stand by Alex, knowing he had lied to me, as he underwent chemotherapy. I am very disappointed at the way things turned out, but I am no longer angry. I have made peace with my soul, knowing for certain that Alex was not the man for me. I will forever shout it from the mountain top that my loving Father, God, protected me and my integrity. My **second wind** brought with it a level of clarity and understanding about how God protected me from Alex. On the wings of **my second wind** came my dream job and an opportunity to study for my MBA.

I firmly believe that relationships can be wonderful, especially with the right person. It's important to take the time to truly get to know someone before committing to them. Too often, we rush into relationships, particularly after a period of loneliness or while rebounding from one that didn't work out. For me, what has been effective is stepping back to reflect on my actions, emotions, and reactions following a breakup—focusing on what I can control.

Having honest conversations with God about your feelings and the relationship can be incredibly helpful. He will guide you in the right direction and ultimately toward the right relationship. Learning to forgive yourself, rediscover self-love, and enjoy your own company is a powerful remedy for healing after a breakup.

Above all, never give up on yourself. Lean on your faith, friends, and family—they'll always be there to support you.

DELIVERED FROM THE VALLEY OF THE UNKNOWN

Finding my Identity

LISA RICHMOND

When asked to describe myself in a single word or to articulate who I am, I often feel stuck, as the task seems overwhelming and impossible. I sift through my experiences in search of a term that truly encapsulates ME—a word that embodies Lisa Richmond. However, I hesitate to settle on one because I believe it's the personal stories of an individual (rather than mere labels), that genuinely define them. My struggles, victories, and dreams are the core elements that have molded me into the person I am today.

Before I embraced the name Lisa Richmond, I was known as Lisa Brantley. I'm divorced from my husband, who gave me his surname, but I hold onto it because the name Lisa Richmond is profoundly meaningful to me. My ex-husband's mother wanted me to abandon it after he got sick and walked out on me, but I had fought for my marriage and my family. I'd fought to pick myself back up again after my husband left me penniless. After all the hard work I did as Lisa Richmond, I refused to leave my name behind.

As a kid, I was smart and had ambition. I wanted to be a singer someday and memorized all the commercial jingles I heard on TV. But I grew up in a highly dysfunctional and abusive household. I've found it challenging to discuss my past and often felt ashamed of my origins. I have struggled with feeling inadequate due to the instability of my home life growing up. That, coupled with the absence of a high school education, left me feeling incomplete. When I was a child, my father battled alcoholism, and my mother faced physical disabilities and mental health challenges. Arguments erupted between my parents frequently, and there were distressing moments when my father physically harmed my mother in front of me and my siblings. We grew up deprived of the love and nurturing typically found in what most would consider to be a normal childhood, which, in turn, perpetuated the dysfunction and abuse we witnessed. We often lacked proper clothing, sharing what little we had and enduring teasing from other kids for being "dirty."

My family moved often because my dad squandered the money for bills on gambling, cigarettes, and alcohol. As a result, our utilities were routinely shut off, leaving us without electricity, heat, water, and sometimes, even food. This disordered lifestyle drove me to seek companionship early on. I longed to escape the turmoil I was experiencing at home and was exhausted from the dysfunction surrounding me. I just wanted to get away and make it all stop.

I met a handsome young man when we were both attending Lake View High School, and one day he asked me out. I turned him down. Although he seemed nice, I didn't know him, so I wasn't comfortable saying yes to a date. After that, we started talking more, and when he asked me to prom, I accepted. Being with him provided an escape from my dysfunctional family environment, so I began dating him. Soon after we began dating on a regular basis, both my parents developed serious illnesses.

My six older siblings weren't willing to take on the responsibility for our parents' care. I was the oldest of the kids at home, so they decided I should drop out of school to support my mother. I didn't feel I had a choice, so I dropped out of school and spent a year caregiving for my mother. The school informed me that I had to leave school the day I turned 19, and if I wanted a high school diploma, by law, I had to attend an alternative school. I was upset but decided to enroll anyway, determined to earn my diploma. However, when I got to the class, I felt intimidated by the other students. I was fearful because they were throwing up gang signs and seemed tough. I didn't feel I belonged there, and I definitely didn't fit in, so I left. Shortly after that, I became pregnant and my whole world took a drastic shift.

My parents were still abusive, and what I thought was a horrible nightmare turned out to be my harsh reality. At such a young age, I was confronted with the difficult truth--I was about to become a young mother with no education, no career, no support, no nothing!

My boyfriend and I found minimum-wage jobs and got married. During one of my father's drunken rages, he became violent, threw me out of the house, and tossed my clothes into the mud beside me. Despite my husband's efforts to reason with him, it was clear we had no choice but to leave. We were fortunate to stay with one of my siblings for a while, and after I gave birth to my daughter, Simone, my husband and I decided to return home. At that point, my father appeared somewhat stable, so we felt it was safe to stay there again.

After months of searching for answers about my baby girl's health, I found myself in the ER with Simone on Christmas Eve. She needed to have emergency brain surgery to treat hydrocephalus, a procedure so critical that a surgeon had to be flown in from Canada. Simone survived the operation, but the doctors warned us she might face developmental delays. Every night, I prayed with all my heart, asking God to protect her and give her a chance at a normal childhood.

It felt as though the dark cloud hanging over us grew heavier with each passing minute. At one point, I was told my daughter wouldn't live to see her fifth birthday—a thought that terrified me. But by the grace of God, she proved the doctors wrong! We faced countless challenges, especially the financial strain brought on by Simone's illness. Navigating government benefits was especially difficult, as it seemed there was little support for families like ours, raising a child with special needs. There were moments when I felt completely lost and on the brink of giving up, but I knew I had to keep moving forward.

A year later, I found myself pregnant again—a situation I was unprepared for. I was not ready to have another child, but my husband had forced himself on me. I gave birth to a boy, but heartbreakingly, he passed away just a few hours later. I vividly recall visiting the doctor the weekend before going into labor, and he reassured me that everything was fine. The tragic loss of my child plunged me into a depression so deep I was unable to even speak about it. The trauma of my husband's actions, combined with the loss of my child, left me shattered, but fate often operates in mysterious ways.

Just when I thought the weight of my anguish was unbearable, my husband fell ill. We sought help from countless doctors, but none could determine the cause of his condition. I felt desperately alone and pleaded with God for guidance. My path seemed shrouded in darkness and uncertainty, but eventually my husband was diagnosed with lymphoma and lupus. The treatments took a heavy toll on his health—causing his teeth to fall out and leaving him too weak to provide for his family. I reassured him that I hadn't married him for his income but because I loved him, and I promised we would overcome together. Yet, four years later, he walked out on me. I made an appeal to my siblings to help me, but none of them came to my rescue.

I was exhausted but somehow found the strength to pack up and move to Waukegan, Illinois. My sister lived there and was doing well, so I felt it was a safe place for me to start over. For seven years, I cut off communication with my family, believing it would provide relief, but after a while, I was really missing them. I felt profoundly alone and struggled to overcome the traumatic events I had endured over the years. Every day, I grappled with questions like, "Why does my confusion and conflict persist? Why can't I find peace within myself?" At times, I even wondered if a curse had befallen my family. The sense of abandonment and the betrayal I felt weighed heavily on me. All I wanted was to have my husband back and return to a normal life, but nothing about my situation with him felt normal. I couldn't understand why he left us so abruptly.

After years of emotional pain, I had finally allowed myself to love again, only to realize my trust had been misplaced. This new love was someone who had been my refuge from past hurts, but after some time he left as well. And when he left, it plunged me into an even deeper depression. Once more, I found myself alone, and I turned to painkillers to numb the pain I felt inside. I seemed to be fading away, drifting away from my body. I lost my identity and my self-worth.

I sought temporary refuge with my family, but the situation quickly escalated to physical violence within days. Desperate for shelter, I reached out to my husband's mother. I explained that my family had assaulted me, and she graciously offered me a place to stay. As grateful as I was for her intervention, my nights there were soon filled with dread. My father-in-law began making inappropriate advances, causing me to barricade my door with a chair to divert his nightly visits. I was too frightened to sleep and stayed awake to watch the door. One evening, he left a note on my bed professing his feelings for me. Bewildered and confused, my reality still felt more like a nightmare.

Seeking comfort, because I didn't have the strength to face my struggles alone, I entered into several abusive relationships (one right after the other) which left me questioning whether I would ever heal. When would the knight on the white horse, who existed only in my imagination, arrive to rescue me? The truth was, there was no savior coming; the only person capable of saving me was myself.

After entering another relationship and welcoming my youngest daughter, Maria, my life seemed to be getting better. Although her father was kind, he cheated on me often. It's easy for some to say, "Just leave him if he doesn't treat you right," but a lack of self-esteem makes a simple action seem like an uphill battle that can take years. The painkillers I was taking, and the deep depression was contributing greatly to the decline in my health. I weighed about 300 pounds, which was compounded by a series of health issues. At the time, I had no idea where to turn or what to do. I felt trapped in my own mind, engulfed in a spiritual battle, and I knew the only way for change to happen was for me to take action. However, I lacked the courage to leave my partner because my daughter, Maria, needed stability.

That may not have been a valid excuse to stay, but I often reflected on my mother's struggles with my father. Did she, too, remain with her man for the sake of their children? Why couldn't I choose to leave my partner? I was scared of loneliness, rejection, and abandonment by everything and everyone. I believed my current relationship was different from the others I'd had, but I couldn't deny the similarities. I was seeking love in all the wrong places when it was within me all along.

Although my husband and I were separated, we maintained a relationship because of our daughter Simone. One day, I got a call that he was in the hospital, and before I could get there to say my last goodbye, he passed away from his illness. That was another devastating blow to me as he was my first love despite the roller coaster relationship we had.

In the midst of those dark moments, I just wanted to disappear, but somewhere, deep inside, a flicker of hope remained. I heard a whisper that told me I could reclaim my life, and I leaned into that whisper.

In 2011, on that Labor Day weekend, I developed a blood clot in my right calf. The doctor prescribed warfarin and sent me home, but the situation got worse. I developed dry eye (at least that's what I believed at the time). The pain in my eye became excruciating, and as I sat in the emergency room, I was thankful that the doctors had given me painkillers that were beginning to kick in. Suddenly, I went blind in that eye. After that, I spent two weeks in quarantine, fighting a meningitis infection that was threatening to take my eye. I prayed to God for something that could take years--a corneal transplant. "What will I do now?" I cried. In my heart, I heard the answer: "I will show you."

I began physical therapy to relearn everyday skills like reading and driving. My fiancé, at the time, left me. Another painful reality I had to face amid my illness. But the following January, I got my transplant and thanked God for his loving gift of returning my eyesight. That experience gave me a **second wind**.

I decided to begin therapy to unpack past trauma and gradually peel back the layers to get to the root of what shaped me. I began to confront the demons of my past, learning that healing is not a linear process. I felt resistance, but pushed through it, step by step, and embraced vulnerability, gaining an understanding that sharing my story generates a source of strength. That revelation caused me to begin writing and pouring my heart into poetry and essays. I became revived and saw each word as a step toward reclaiming my narrative. Writing became my refuge, transforming my pain into art, and helping me confront the shadows of my past. I discovered how storytelling has the power to connect us across distances and experiences.

As I became more involved in my community, volunteering in shelters and community centers, it sparked hope in others and ignited a sense of purpose in me. The connections I formed as I began to reach out beyond myself reminded me that we are never truly alone. My story began to weave into the fabric of others, and together, we forged a path toward healing.

I focused on creating an environment where my daughters felt safe to express themselves. I wanted to break the cycle of dysfunction, giving them the childhood I had longed for. We talked openly about our fears and dreams, and I encouraged them to chase their passions.

My scars, once a source of shame, have been transformed into symbols of survival. I celebrate the woman I am becoming, set boundaries, and demand the respect I deserve. I have learned how to advocate for my needs and surrounded myself with a supportive community of people who lift me up.

The journey of healing is ongoing, but I no longer feel defined by my past. In the past, when asked to describe myself in a single word or to articulate who I am, I often found myself at a loss for words. Today, I embrace the complexities of my identity, standing tall in the face of adversity. Today, I know who I am. I am Lisa Richmond—a survivor, a mother, a storyteller because God gave **me a second wind.**

THE BOW AND ARROW COVENANT

Rising from Resistance

DR. JOAN T RANDALL

Rocky Road

The clock on my laptop ticked toward midnight, its digital glow is the only light piercing the darkness of my small, silent home office. As the last seconds of 2022 vanished, I felt an overwhelming heaviness wrap around my heart, breaking it into pieces I wasn't sure I could put back together. The loneliness was suffocating, like a blanket of emptiness draped over walls that once held memories of joy and love.

Suddenly, the tears came—a torrent I couldn't control. It was only minutes into January 2023, and I was utterly and completely alone. I had never spent a New Year's Eve like that one —without family, without friends, without a single voice to welcome the promise of a new beginning. I reached for my phone, desperately hoping for a missed call or a forgotten text, but the screen was blank. No one had reached out, and I could almost hear the mocking silence that followed each unanswered ring in my mind.

My pride kept me from making the first move, telling myself I'd reach out later. But deep down, the reality stung—my world felt empty, void of the love I once knew. The surgery from just a week earlier had left me physically fragile, but it was the sudden isolation that left me emotionally shattered. I wept, not just for that moment, but for all I had lost—my parents who had passed on, the marriage that had ended only months previously, and the children and grandchildren who were far away from me at that moment.

I wept for the woman I had been, the one who built a life of success and stability, only to watch it crumble beneath her feet. I once had it all—the home, the partner, the comfort of financial security, and the luxury that masked the deeper voids. As I sat in the darkness of my office and in the darkness of that moment, despair joined me there. It was a familiar foe; one I hadn't encountered in years. The darkness of my thoughts grew darker still, and the abyss felt bottomless.

As my thoughts spiraled downward, a voice from deep within jolted me back, saying, "No, Joan! God didn't bring you this far to abandon you!"

The words echoed like a lifeline, yanking me from the darkest corners of my mind. I repeated them aloud, allowing them to break the grip of despair. I took a shaky breath, then another, letting each one remind me, "*I am still here, still breathing, still alive.*"

By the time I gathered enough strength to rise from my chair, the clock read 2:30 a.m. I grabbed my walker, a stark reminder of my vulnerability, and shuffled to my bedroom. The tears still flowed, but they were quieter, less consuming. As I lay down, the pillow catching my silent grief, I prayed for the strength to keep going, and as sleep finally claimed me, I whispered to the darkness, "This isn't how my story ends."

Rescue

The familiar buzz of an incoming text message jolted me from my restless sleep, pulling me out of the darkness that surrounded my room. I reached blindly for my glasses, eager to see who would be texting me so early. As my eyes adjusted to the phone's glow, I noticed it was just past 6:00 a.m. The message was from my sister-friend, Tamra. Attached was a YouTube video, but it was her words beneath the link that gripped my attention.

"Watch when you have time," she cautioned. "It's three hours long."

Curiosity tugged at me harder than sleep ever could, especially after the haunting events of the night before. My heart was heavy, the memories still raw, but I needed a distraction—something to keep the darkness at bay. I clicked on the link, letting the video load as I wrestled against the flood of painful memories that threatened to drown me once more. Little did Tamra know; her text was no ordinary text—it was divine intervention. Yahweh was reaching out to me through her, through a video. He saw my brokenness, my silent pleas for relief from the crushing weight of past adversities.

As I watched the video, each scripture and every spoken word seeped into my soul, filling the empty, aching spaces with a sense of overflow I hadn't felt in years. For three uninterrupted hours, I stayed transfixed, absorbing everything as though it were sustenance for my weary spirit. By the end, I sat on my bed, overwhelmed, but my tears were not tears of despair. They were tears of repentance and a flood of gratitude.

I repented for all the ways I had disappointed Elohim—for my faltering faith, my fear, my pride, and every sin known and unknown. I laid bare my soul, admitting my erratic thoughts, my neglect in giving God my best, my failure to be a good steward, and my selfish grasping for His glory. Amid the weeping and worship, I found myself whispering a plea. *"Teach me to be a Bride of Christ, to silence the noise within, to know you in an intimate way."*

I asked Him to lift the shame and the pain that had become so familiar, and to free me from the cycles I kept finding myself in. "Have I learned this time?" I questioned. The lesson felt different, yet the circumstances remained painfully the same. I knew deep down that real change had to start within me.

After what seemed like hours, I finally stood up, wiping away the remnants of my tears. I sent my family a quick "Happy New Year," then found myself standing before the mirror.

"Here I am again, Lord," I whispered (my reflection blurred by fresh tears.) "What do you want me to see?"

Reflection

The Lord led me back to a glimpse of the life I had fled just four months prior. The legacy I once built for my children had vanished, lost to financial hardship. The marriage I believed would last a lifetime had crumbled. Love had faded, replaced by resentment and silence, leaving us as two strangers in the same house, each charting a separate course. Our mismatched beliefs created a spiritual divide, and financial secrets and a lack of shared budgeting made it impossible to manage money effectively. I was a lonely wife in a loveless home where my husband occasionally slept in our bed with headphones on. After seventeen years of being together, the latter three years were a roller coaster of uncertainties. I felt isolated, unloved, and deeply unhappy.

I was eighty pounds overweight and on the brink of diabetes, which added to my distress. After being on medication for over 15 years, I was unsuccessful in controlling my blood pressure. Earlier that year, I suffered a transient ischemic attack (minor stroke) and realized I had reached a breaking point. It was very apparent to me that staying in that marriage might cost me my life, so, I made the choice to leave. When I left, I took my clothes, books, a dresser, and a nightstand. I was going to start over from square one.

I found a small townhouse apartment in a neighborhood about five miles from my previous home. At fifty-eight years old, it was the first time I had ever lived alone. I had walked away from everything, and my savings were depleted. I felt abandoned, unprotected, and without provision. I found myself feeling like a failure.

Ninety days after leaving my husband, I underwent surgery to remove a grapefruit-sized tumor from my left thigh. Complications arose when the drain inserted at the surgical site became infected, leading to a painful bout of cellulitis. It was a trying time. I stayed with my sister for about six days following the surgery, and she provided much-needed care and encouragement during those dark days. I often found myself in tears, overwhelmed by the emptiness I felt. When I finally returned to my apartment, it was December 30th—just one day before my breaking point.

Reality

I focused my gaze back to the girl in the mirror, and as I looked deeply into my own eyes, I allowed myself to confront the person staring back at me. I wasn't just seeing my reflection; I was seeing my reality—raw, vulnerable, and unfiltered. The puffiness around my eyes spoke of countless nights lost to tears and silent prayers, but in that moment, the mirror was more than a surface—it became a window into my soul.

My mind replayed the video's message that Tamra had sent, each word echoing like a call to rise again. It was as if the Holy Spirit's voice resonated in my heart, not with condemnation, but with the warmth of hope and an invitation to come closer. I placed my hands on the cool surface of the mirror, not out of self-pity, but as a gesture of surrender.

"Teach me, Lord," I whispered, *"how to love this person you created—me."*

It felt like a bold request, almost foreign. I had spent so much time being double minded with words and beliefs, but there I was, daring to ask for restoration. I wanted God's eyes to be my lens. What did He see? What potential had He placed within me that had been buried under the weight of life's disappointments and failures?

I remembered the words of the video speaker: "God can only work with what we're willing to give Him." That truth hit me hard. How much had I really given over to Him? In that instant, I knew I needed to be real with God, not with polished prayers, but with raw honesty.

"Lord, I give you my broken pieces," I said aloud, my voice barely steady. *"I'm tired of pretending to be whole when I know I'm shattered."*

Suddenly, the room felt heavy, not with despair, but with the presence of God's grace. It was as if Yahweh had stepped right into that small space, meeting me in my vulnerability. The tears came again, as a release, a cleansing of all that had been held back for too long. It wasn't just a cry of sadness, but one of hope—a deep yearning to be filled anew.

Then, in the stillness of that sacred moment, a memory emerged—one I had pushed aside for years. It was a reminder of a promise I had made to God years ago, during another difficult season. *"If you bring me out of this, Lord, I will serve you wholeheartedly."*

I meant it back then, but life had gotten complicated, and the promise had become lost in the noise of daily survival. That memory wasn't an accusation; it was a call back to my true self, the self I was meant to be. It was as if Yahweh was saying, "I haven't forgotten your promise, and neither have I forgotten mine."

With a sense of urgency, I went to my bedroom, grabbed my journal from the nightstand, sat on the bed and began to write—no eloquent words, just the raw thoughts pouring from my heart. It was a prayer, a declaration, and a renewal of my commitment.

"Lord, I am yours. All of me, broken and flawed. Teach me to walk in purpose not just for me, but for your glory. Let my story be a testimony of your grace and power."

As the ink flowed, I felt a shift inside me. It wasn't a grand transformation; it was subtle, like the first rays of dawn breaking through the darkness. It was a renewal, a resurgence, and it was real. I knew the journey ahead wouldn't be easy, but I also knew I wasn't alone. Yahweh had always been there, waiting for me to see what He saw—a beloved child, worthy of redemption and purpose.

When I closed the journal, I felt a sense of peace, not because everything was suddenly perfect, but because I had made a decision—a decision to stand, to move forward, and to embrace the calling that had never left me. I also knew I needed to fix every area of my life, the physical, emotional, and the mental. I felt courage rise from my feet all the way up to my heart.

Ready

A new psychological reflection of me emerged, and it was different. I didn't just see the scars of my past, I saw a woman who was ready to fight for her future, not in her own strength, but in His. "*Thank you, El Roi.*" I whispered, "*for seeing me, for loving me, and for choosing me despite it all.*"

I was ready for a new journey. There was work to be done, lessons to be learned, and a story to tell—a story of grace, healing, and the unrelenting love of God. The kind of story that, one day, I would share with others, not just as a tale of redemption but as an invitation to let God write theirs, too. Yahweh allowed me to be stripped of everything so I could be rebuilt as His bride. Like an archer pulling back the bowstring to its limit, He drew me in to capture my full attention and succeeded.

A surprise visit from my sister-friend Erika to my new apartment became the unexpected lifeline I didn't know I needed. What started as a simple gathering, evolved into a five-hour deliverance session where I fully submitted to God. I repented, denounced old ties, forgave past hurts, broke every generational curse, and renewed my covenant with God. With fasting and fervent prayer, I sought guidance, and God delivered—leading me to complete restoration.

I prioritized my physical health and shed over forty pounds. I got off all medications that had defined my life for years. Foods that once harmed me lost their appeal and my heart grew stronger, like it was in my youth. Every morning, I began with praise, worship, prayer, and a deep dive into the Word of God. I soon realized that solitude was God's way of setting me apart, teaching, and revealing His character to me. I prayed for the fruits of the Spirit to fill me, and He answered, transforming my home into His sanctuary. Peace flowed through every room, faith became my strength, and His Word nourished me. Scriptures took on fresh, revelatory meaning. I let go of anything that did not align with the Holy Spirit and my renewed identity. A deep, indescribable joy settled within me.

Two years later, here I am living in *MY* **second wind**. The bowstrings were pulled as far back as God could take them—not for a restart, but for a new beginning, orchestrated by His hand. He has released the arrow of His promises, allowing me to soar. For every pain, He provided purpose, and for every resistance, He enabled me to rise. From the ashes of shame, He gave me gold. From the emptiness within, He filled me with His light, His name, and His calling.

Restoration

In September 2023, I had the privilege of co-hosting a mission trip to Kenya with thirteen dedicated missionaries. During that impactful journey, 1,100 souls accepted Christ. My memoir, *Bags in The Attic*, not only won an international award, but was also pitched for a screenplay. Additionally, *The Image in the Mirror Anthology*, co-authored by twenty talented individuals, received international acclaim, winning the award for best anthology.

My business, Victorious You Press, was further blessed with an investor who joined as an active leader, taking on the role of Chief Operations Officer. We also achieved full registration as a Minority Women Business Enterprise, expanding our capacity to engage and do business with the city, state, and corporate entities in North Carolina.

On a personal note, my oldest daughter earned her Brokers-In-Charge License and launched her own commercial real estate property management company. Meanwhile, my youngest celebrated a well-deserved promotion to Operations Supervisor at a branch of one of the largest banking institutions in North Carolina.

Most recently, I was honored to receive an Honorary Doctorate in Humane Letters, along with a Global Fellowship in Leadership and Business.

This is truly *your* bow and arrow season, Dr. Joan Elizabeth Thaxter Randall!

ABOUT THE AUTHORS

NIKEMA BRYANT

Nikema "Kema" Bryant Nikema was born the oldest of four girls in Philadelphia, PA. She was educated in the Philadelphia School District until moving to South Carolina her sophomore year of high school. After losing her only child in 2021 to an act of senseless gun violence, she has become an advocate for grieving mothers. She co-founded Team 55, a non-profit organization that focuses on giving back to the community through scholarships and donations, all while keeping the legacy alive of her only child.

ANGELA M MITCHELL

Angela M Mitchell is an Award-Winning International Best-Selling Author, International Speaker, Digital Marketing Strategist, Brand Marketing Coach, and CEO of Back to Her. She empowers women to reignite their passions, rediscover their purpose, reinvent themselves and their businesses. She teaches them how to leverage digital and content marketing to build a solid digital presence and position their companies for long-term growth.

Since overcoming her challenges with bipolar disorder, anxiety, and depression, it has become her mission to inspire other women to get to the other side of their mental and emotional health challenges as well. You can connect with her at back2her.org.

KRISTY BUSIJA

Long before becoming the award-winning CEO of Next Conversation Consulting and a Forbes contributor, Kristy Busija was always the go-to expert for turning chaos into clarity. Whether it was navigating organizational challenges or resolving complex problems, she saw puzzles where others saw confusion. Known for her ability to transform disorder into actionable, strategic solutions, Kristy has consistently helped organizations create cultures where employees are not only productive but genuinely engaged. With a keen eye for detail and a results-driven mindset, she empowers leaders to build workplaces that foster both innovation and collaboration.

CHARMAINE LAFONDÉ

Charmaine LaFondé is an author and speaker who is enthusiastic about using her writing to inspire hope, encouragement, and a more optimistic mindset. At 62, Charmaine found inspiration to write and publish her first book after hearing about her son's death on Facebook. "From Grief to Gratitude: A 31-day Devotional Guide to Greater Peace" is her latest book where she shares the principles she used to overcome grief. Affectionately dubbed the "Queen of F.A.R.T.S" which means, *Find A Reason To Smile*, she currently resides in Florida with her husband and best friend, Amos Castillo.

CHRISTAL SPENCE NEWKIRK

Christal Spence Newkirk is a 2X Bestselling Author, Executive Coach, CEO of ACS, a division of AboveHR that partners with major organizations to provide general construction and facilities maintenance services.

Christal is the Georgia Chapter President for QC Women in Business effective Jan 1, 2025. QCWIB helps women-owned business suppliers connect faster with B2B & Corporate contracts.

Christal has over 20 years of Corporate Recruitment & DEI experience. She earned her Master of Science Management degree and bachelor's degree from North Carolina State University.

Christal and her husband, Rodney are CoPreneurs and currently reside in Fort Mill, SC.

SHARON R THOMPSON

Sharon R Thompson owns OneSource Logistic Solutions, LLC, a support service for commercial drivers that she started in 2021. She is also the Capital Admin (Project Assistant) at Atrium Health, where she has been employed for seven years. Born in New York City and raised in Charlotte, NC, Sharon holds an Associate in Science and a Bachelor of Business Administration from Montreat College.

She loves the beach and travel. Her passion is serving others and spending time with those she loves. Sharon has been a lead usher at her church for nine years and has participated in several mission trips in her local community. She is a woman of standards, values, morals, and integrity and a budding author and entrepreneur. She is a mother of three and Noni (grandmother of six + three bonus).

LESLIE J COTTRELL

Leslie J Cottrell, Book-Writing Coach, serves as Chief Operating Officer at Victorious You Press. Leslie is a two-time best-selling author. She has extensive experience in senior leadership roles in restaurants and hospitality and served as the Food and Beverage Director for a nationwide events company. While counseling her mother through her dad's decline she found there was no single source of information to aid families in planning for life's contingencies. Following her father's death, she wrote that book. This led to a shift in her professional focus. Her favorite role is as a book-writing coach. She delights in assisting new and almost new authors on their writing journey. Her style of writing coaching takes an author from book idea to publication submission. Her goal is to support authors in a way that allows them the freedom to dig deeper into their writing. She lives on the seacoast in New Hampshire.

REGINA NICHELLE

Regina Nichelle is an entrepreneur, philanthropist, strategist, and change catalyst fueled by passion to empower others. As the owner of Transformation Coaching & Consulting, she has become a trusted guide in leadership, change management, and personal development, helping individuals and organizations achieve meaningful and lasting transformation.

Regina's passion for uplifting others is rooted in her own journey of overcoming challenges, including the loss of a child, divorce and single motherhood. Inspired by her experiences, she founded the 501(c)(3) nonprofit *Mpowerd*, in 2020. Through this organization, she reaches women across the US and Canada on her mission to encourage, educate and equip single mothers to create strong futures for themselves and their families.

The devoted mother to Zachary and servant of God, Regina finds joy in music, great food, fine wine, and travel. Through her work and her story, Regina continues to inspire women to embrace their potential, redefine their futures, and lead lives full of possibility.

ROBIN A. HILL

Joy Specialist, author and motivational speaker, Robin Angela Hill is a multifaceted woman who loves God. She is the mother of 2 beautiful daughters and grandmother of 5 loved grandchildren. Licensed to minister in 1993, Robin also developed JDT Christian Academy from K-4-12th grade. There she served for14 years. Her family relocated to NC in 2007 and started a church. In 2009, Robin separated and then divorced in 2010. She met Alonzo Hill in 2014 and they married in 2015. Together they founded three businesses (zolingosspiceforlife.com, wellnesstodayinsideout.com and spiceforlifeworldtravel.com).

She founded the Lady Lexus Club in 2022. In 2023 after 9 years, she retired from Hendrick Lexus in Charlotte. In 2023, she also recorded her song *"That's Why I Praise You"*. Robin authored *"The*

Making of a Beast", "52 Weeks of Purposeful Thinking", "Grown Folks Business/Marriage Can Work", co-authored "Life Is a Process for Progress" and "Urban Joy Ever-After" Coming-Soon!.

SARA OMAYA AGAK

Sara Omaya Agak is an accomplished professional with over 15 years of experience in clinical, supply chain, and regulatory affairs in the pharmaceutical sector in Nairobi, Kenya.

She holds a Bachelor's in Pharmacy from the Nelson Mandela Metropolitan University in South Africa and is pursuing her Master's in Business Administration at Strathmore University in Nairobi, Kenya. Sara is a Director of the Board of The Nairobi Hospice in Nairobi, Kenya, and a former Director of the Pharmacy and Poisons Board in Kenya.

She enjoys coaching and mentoring young adults and believes in empowering people to be and do more. Sara is an avid reader, loves to travel, and enjoys her Thursday evenings immensely.

LISA RICHMOND

Lisa Richmond is a certified Life Coach and Recovery Coach based in Lake County, Illinois, specializing in mental health and addiction recovery. As a licensed QPR Gatekeeper instructor, she is committed to suicide prevention and raising awareness about trauma and violence in communities. Drawing from her personal experiences in a dysfunctional family, Lisa empowers individuals to overcome challenges and build self-esteem.

Currently pursuing a Bachelor of Science in Addiction Counseling, she is the founder of Identity.Me Inc. and Transformational.Me LLC. Lisa holds multiple certifications, including Certified Trauma Coach and Certified Domestic Violence Advocate, underscoring her dedication to supporting others on their healing journeys. Through her coaching and advocacy efforts, Lisa aims to foster resilience and promote personal growth, making a meaningful impact on the lives of those she serves.

Dr. JOAN T RANDALL

Dr. Joan T Randall is president of Joan T. Randall Enterprise LLC, founder of Victorious You Press, and creator of Book 2 Business & Beyond®. She is a highly accomplished, award-winning independent publisher, internationally recognized speaker, and award-winning multi-best-selling author. As a publisher, Joan helps entrepreneurs and mission-driven leaders turn their stories into powerful tools for impact and influence. Her exceptional work has earned her numerous awards and accolades regionally and internationally. Joan has been featured on major networks and listed as a Career-Mastered Top Entrepreneurial Woman to Watch in 2023 and the Career-Mastered 2025 recipient of the Leadership In Action award.

Joan received a Women's Entrepreneurship Certificate from Cornell University, a Certificate in Homiletics from Howard University, and a Certificate in Christian Leadership from Global Impact University and an Honorary Doctorate in DLitt, with a Global Fellowship in Leadership Principles from Mainseed Christian University.

Her memoir Bags in The Attic won the Gold First Place Award in the BookFest Spring 2024 Award.

Dr. Joan was born in Kingston, Jamaica, and resides in Charlotte, NC.

www.ingramcontent.com/pod-product-compliance
Lightning Source LLC
Chambersburg PA
CBHW071754120626
46550CB00002B/785